ISRAEL: The Changing National Agenda

Israel
The Changing National Agenda

AVRAM SCHWEITZER

CROOM HELM
London • Sydney • Dover, New Hampshire

In association with *The Jerusalem Institute for Israel Studies*

© 1986 Jerusalem Institute for Israel Studies
Croom Helm Ltd, Provident House, Burrell Row,
Beckenham, Kent BR3 1AT
Croom Helm Australia Pty Ltd, Suite 4, 6th Floor,
64–76 Kippax Street, Surry Hills, NSW 2010, Australia

British Library Cataloguing in Publication Data

Schweitzer, Avraham
    Israel: the changing national agenda.
    1. Israel —— Politics and government
    —— 1948
    I. Title
    956.94′05   DS126.5

    ISBN 0-7099-3382-7

Croom Helm, 51 Washington Street, Dover,
New Hampshire 03820, USA

Library of Congress Cataloging-in-Publication Data

Schweitzer, Avraham, 1923-   .
    Israel: the changing national agenda.

    Translation of: Mahpakhim.
    Includes index.
    1. Israel–politics and government. 2. Mifleget
po'ale erets–Yiśra' el. 3. Likud (party) 4. Dayan,
moshe, 1915-   . 5. Begin, Menachem, 1913-   .
I. Title.
DS126.S3613   1986   320.95694   86-6220
ISBN 0-7099-3382-7

This publication was made possible by funds granted by the Charles H. Revson
Foundation of New York to the Jerusalem Institute for Israel Studies. The
statements made and the views expressed, are solely the responsibility of the
authors.

Phototypeset by Sunrise Setting, Torquay, Devon
Printed and bound in Great Britain by Mackays of Chatham Ltd, Kent

CONTENTS

INTRODUCTION

The Coming of Likud

The defeat of the Labour government at the polls on 17 May 1977 signalled an upheaval in Israeli politics. The overthrow of Labour is said to have produced a fundamental political change: the subjection of national priorities to a new central theme — the *de facto* imposition of state sovereignty over the entire area of western Palestine. A new governing coalition had come into being, the nucleus of which was the ultra-nationalist Herut Party[1] led by Menachem Begin. This was expected to be a long-term heir to the coalition headed by Mapai (*Mifleget Poalei Israel* or the Palestine Workers' Party), which had first led the *Yishuv*, the Jewish settlement in Palestine, from 1931 until the establishment of the state in 1948, and afterwards Israel for twenty nine years and two days — ever since that momentous Friday afternoon, 14 May 1948, when David Ben-Gurion proclaimed the rebirth of Jewish independence in the historic homeland.

All this and more has been said about the upheaval; what has not been said, however, is that it came seventeen years too late. In 1960 Mapai, Israel's ruling party *par excellence*, ground to a halt, having more or less accomplished the programme it had set itself. An internal crisis tore the leadership apart in a matter of a few weeks, casting doubt upon the inner cohesion of the party and upon the authority of the man who then stood at the helm and guaranteed both its stability and the stability of its rule: David Ben-Gurion. If conditions had been ripe, that is to say, if Mapai had then faced an opposition capable of governing the country, the fifth Knesset elections in August 1961 might have brought about the party's downfall and seen its national leadership replaced by that of another major party.

That is not what happened. The axe stopped just short of Mapai's head and the crisis passed, leaving the party much weakened. It split in 1965, and then in 1966 it had to face a profound economic recession during which 100,000 Israelis became unemployed. Bitter jokes became current, best summed up by the sign which was

1

supposed to be hung at Lod airport, 'Last one out, please turn off the lights', hinting that Mapai's overthrow was merely a matter of time. Just then, however, war broke out, ending in a shattering victory over the combined Egyptian, Syrian, and Jordanian armed forces. In its aftermath Israelis remained loyal to the government which had overcome the threat to national existence. The euphoria of victory, enhanced by the strange and enchanting atmosphere of the conquered territories on the West Bank, the Sinai Peninsula, and the Golan Heights, contributed to the restabilisation of the regime, despite the cost of retaining those territories, the primary cost being 492 dead and 1739 wounded between 12 June, 1967 and 3 May 1972, when sporadic fighting with the Syrians ceased on the Northern Front.

The Yom Kippur War once again shook the public's faith in the government's military superiority. Had the country not been beset by a deep shock following the surprise of Yom Kippur, it might well have settled accounts with its worn-out leaders in the elections of 31 December 1973. However, once again they were granted a period of grace, another term of office. Under Labour Party leadership, the government which assumed power during the summer of 1974 tried manfully to cope with a legacy of accumulated failure and fatigue. Notwithstanding its brave fight against waste and corruption, Labour could no longer conceal the bankruptcy of its political programme, and, in the end, it was defeated.

Nevertheless the results of the elections for the ninth Knesset, which brought Menachem Begin's Likud to power with a convincing plurality (his list received 43 seats, as against 32 for the Labour list), were unexpected. In *Basic Surprise*[2], a book dealing with the surprise of Yom Kippur, Dr Tswi Lanir distinguishes between two sorts of surprise: situational and basic. In the case of the 1977 elections, the surprise was certainly basic. The rule of Mapai, and afterwards of the Labour Party or the Labour Alignment, had lasted so long—nearly 46 years if one starts from 1931, the year when representatives of the labour movement took over the main portfolios in the Jewish Agency Executive — that it seemed to be part of the natural environment, like the air, the sun, and the hills in the east. It is characteristic of basic surprises that they are not expected to occur despite manifest signs that they are impending; in other words, people refuse to believe their own eyes. That is what Lanir says in the case of the Yom Kippur War; that is also what occurred in the elections of 1977.

Public opinion polls predicted the results during the months preceding the elections as follows:

	March 1977 %	April 1977 %	13 May 1977 %
Labour	29.7–32.0	25.5–35.0	32.1–26.6
Likud	14.9–29.1	18.1–28.89	31.3–34.0
Dash (Democratic Movement for Change)	8.7–19.0	6.4–13.1	10.1–12.5
NRP (National Religious Party)	2.9–7.5	4.1–7.4	8.00–10.0

As election day drew nearer, the shape of the impending upheaval grew more evident. Labour was falling behind the Likud and the parties which were to prove the nucleus for an alternative coalition: the second column of the final opinion poll was right on target. None the less people were thrown into a state of shock mingled with disbelief at 11 p.m. on the night of 17 May as the television announcers began reading out results taken from sample ballot boxes, a forecasting technique used for the first time in Israel.

The public at large was not alone in being surprised. Dr Eliahu Ben Elissar, one of Begin's closest aides, said that he was not surprised by the results because they had been predicted by a public opinion poll. He added, however, that he and his associates had kept these results in strict secrecy because 'We found it hard to believe them'. On the other hand, Micha Reisser, a Herut activist who later became a Member of the Knesset, placed his faith in the stars, claiming that he was not surprised because a fashionable astrologer had predicted the Likud victory. In the Labour camp the routine reaction was that 'It', meaning the loss of power, 'could not be'. That night Shimon Peres told journalists that he had not expected the results, and that they were 'a painful surprise'.[3]

Immediately after the elections various explanations began to surface as both private citizens and professional politicians tried to explain the political upheaval to themselves. Many people concluded that the main reason was a kind of systemic fatigue within the Labour Party, the result of 29 years of uninterrupted rule, or, rather, of 46 years of power. Others concentrated on specific issues such as the financial corruption in which members of the government and those close to them had been involved. Dr Minna Tsemach, who directed the public opinion poll mentioned above, stated that respondents did refer to the corruption charges brought against Asher Yadlin, the former head of the Histadrut Sick Fund[4] and a candidate for the governorship of the Bank of Israel, saying that it had had a great deal of influence upon them and affected their vote.

Later on another explanation emerged. A more detailed analysis of the election results revealed that Likud reaped its greatest success among Oriental Jewish voters in the ethnic neighbourhoods of the major cities and in the development towns. Some people concluded that Likud had gained a sort of political monopoly (or at least a decisive advantage) among Israeli Jews of Asian and African origin. Others added that, since these voters were a majority of the population, and, moreover, a growing majority because of their higher birth rate, Likud had become the permanent majority party. To anticipate, the results of the 1981 elections were later seen as empirical proof confirming the analysis.

If, however, one gives the matter further thought, it appears doubtful whether the upheaval of May 1977 is attributable either to corruption in high places or to the ethnic factor alone, or in particular. As for the opinion that the Labour Party was exhausted after 46 years in power, this too needs qualification. It was not merely or specifically the passage of time which had eroded the electoral appeal of the Labour Party.

No-one can deny the harmful effect of the manifestations of systemic rot and personal corruption which came to light between 1974 and 1977. Those who claim that it was corruption that brought Labour down concentrate on that period, in which it had become highly visible; however, it is unconvincing to attribute the upheaval of 17 May mainly to the scandals of the three years of Rabin's premiership. The political change which took place after the upheaval was too far-reaching and the rejection of what had been achieved under Labour rule was too comprehensive to be attributed merely to the events of three short years. Moreover, the electoral results do not confirm the thesis that it was the rot and corruption in the government which eroded Labour's electoral support. For it was the Likud which emerged victorious, not the Democratic Movement for Change, the party which advocated clean and efficient government and high individual moral standards.

As for the ethnic factor, upon further reflection, far from explaining the results of the election, it seems to be part of the puzzle. In the past large numbers of Oriental Jews had supported Mapai and assured its consecutive victories at the polls. There were periods such as the 1950s when the residents of the immigrant camps, the new agricultural villages, and the development towns had seen David Ben-Gurion as a messiah who had redeemed them from the exile of Ishmael. To the extent that they were subject to economic distress and feelings of wounded pride deriving from the destruction of their traditions and the severing of family ties — the factors today used to explain the ethnic tension which is said to be one of the identifying marks of Israeli society — at that time these wounds were much fresher and more painful. Poverty was more palpable — many immigrants literally went without their daily bread at times — as was the trauma of immigration and being cut off from an environment which had sustained and nourished the social fabric of the ghettoes from which the new immigrants came. Yet in that catastrophic period of mass immigration, when Jews from Asia and Africa — who, though desperately poor, still had maintained an orderly communal life which drew stability from the family hierarchy and from some sort of economic activity — were turned out of airplanes or ships straight into tents or asbestos barracks, when they barely earned a living from work to which they were unaccustomed, most of the imigrants still supported Mapai. Now their sons and daughters, far better off economically and probably culturally, were the ones who turned their backs on Mapai, manifesting a profound hatred for it and contempt for its achievements. Was that phenomenon then so much to be taken for granted, so self-explanatory that it could be used to account for the upheaval or was it something which itself required explanation?

Similarly, the metaphorical explanation that the Labour Party lost power because of 'metal fatigue' needs further examination. The impression created by that explanation is that in 1977 a party with a worn-out, broken-down old leadership went to the polls, a party whose strength had dwindled away during its decades in power. But the truth was quite different. The government in power at the time of the 1977 downfall was quite fresh and new in Israeli political terms: its leaders, the Prime Minister and the Ministers of Defence, Foreign Affairs, and the Treasury, had served in those offices only since June 1974, less than three years. The Labour Party, which was trounced on 17 May, was less worn-out physically and politically than any government under Mapai since the establishment of the state; it was fresher and more of a new departure even than the government led by Levi Eshkol after the 1965 elections, when Ben-Gurion and his followers were removed from Mapai.

Defining the National Agenda

The average citizen of whatever country works for a living and supports his family: his own welfare, defined broadly, and that of his family are at the centre of his existence and activities. But in a democratic country like Israel the individual also lives and acts as a citizen, that is, as someone who has not only the right but also the obligation to influence the way in which the community is governed. The most common and simple reason offered for this is that the welfare of the individual is bound up with that of the community. (Some theorists argue that the one is derived from the other, but this is not the place to debate definitions. Nevertheless, it may be noted that a person's views in his role as citizen comprise the same elements as his views as a private individual — his self-interest and that of the group closest to him. Because of that identity the transition from a person's opinion as an individual to his opinion as a citizen is so smooth.) The most stable and comprehensive organisation of a community of citizens is the state: the individual, in his role as a citizen, is meant to be an active partner, to the best of his ability, in forming an opinion as to what the state ought to do for the general good and how it ought to proceed. Members of the political community, i.e. organisations such as political parties and their emissaries in the government, or writers in the media, or scholars who deal in social issues, and the like, actively sift out current opinions: what is left in the sieve is public opinion. But that material is still too fluid: the party leaderships must further refine and solidify it, formulating it into proposals for a national agenda. That agenda will then guide the government.

Naturally there is always more than a single proposal for the national agenda. But one is dominant: the one which is formulated by the ruling party (or the governing coalition) and guides it. This agenda also marks out the area within which discussion of public issues takes place. In other words, operational decisions are made in terms of that agenda which generally remains in force for a longer period than a single parliamentary term.

The rule of certain parties is identified with a given national agenda. With the passage of time the national agenda guiding the government gradually and inevitably diverges from present requirements: when that divergence reaches a critical point, the national agenda is replaced by another, sweeping the party identified with it into power. This is what happened, for example during the 1930s in the United States, when Roosevelt took power; and that is what happened in Israel on 17 May 1977.

Notes

1. Initially conservative, militantly anti-socialist, anti-trade union, Herut has become in the last decade very much the party of the poorer classes, while retaining its uncompromising nationalist programme (e.g. total opposition to any territorial concessions in the West Bank).

2. Tswi Lanir, *The Basic Surprise: Intelligence in Crisis* (Hebrew) (Hakibutz Hameuhad, Centre for Strategic Studies, Tel Aviv, 1983).

3. See Ari Avneri, *Hamapolet* (*The Collapse*) (Hebrew) (Revivim, Tel Aviv, 1977).

4. The Histadrut is Israel's major labour federation, and its Sick Fund provides health care for the majority of the population.

1 INITIAL SUCCESSES

The War of Independence and the establishment of a state within a hostile environment naturally, as it were, led to the creation of a certain national agenda: the leading party in the ruling coalition and its leaders, in particular David Ben-Gurion, were easily identified with the needs and tasks which were the order of that day. The state, which seemed to be little more than a word written in the decision of the UN General Assembly of 22 November 1947 setting up the State of Israel, had to be defended. Borders had to be carved out. After effective sovereignty had been achieved by means of war, its institutions had to be installed and their functions defined, a system of legislature and administration had to be established, the armed forces, which had provided the nation with operational sovereignty, had to be organised, and so on. In short, sovereignty had to be given substance. Mapai, having prepared for the task of gaining sovereignty and providing its substance for the past seventeen years, became the governing party with no apparent effort and without having to reaffirm the legitimacy of its leadership: the national agenda and its operational programme, as defined and proposed by its leader, David Ben-Gurion, were accepted by the community as being one and the same thing.

This is the background to the slogan 'statism' used by Ben-Gurion to sum up the national agenda as conceived by Mapai at the time. The identification of the party with the development of the new state did away with the distinction between the ruling party and Israeli sovereignty: having taken charge of the overall as well as the daily administration of the state, members of the party, or people close to it, blurred the boundary between the two. Given the practical identity of the objective needs of the new state and their perception by the party that had most adequately formulated the national agenda, the complaints voiced by Mapai's political rivals about its near monopoly of leadership positions and its thirst for power seemed mere pettifoging: Mapai *was* the state.

Immigration Policy

We must now take a look at the first significant action taken by Mapai. Mass immigration to the new state almost entirely emptied certain places of their Jewish inhabitants: Bulgaria, Yemen, Iraq, and later on North Africa were all effectively cleared of their Jews. In deciding to encourage mass immigration, Mapai was influenced by memories of the Holocaust and by the sense that it had to rescue everyone it could from situations where physical destruction or total assimilation threatened. But pragmatic considerations, response to the needs of a state established in a hostile environment, also guided the Mapai decision-makers. The party leaders did not labour under the delusion that the War of Independence and its aftermath would reconcile the neighbouring Arab states to the new sovereign entity. The numerical disproportion between the population of Israel and that of the neighbouring countries after the war was certainly alarming. Security demanded the rapid population of the country. Assuming that empty territories invited infiltration, and, afterwards, renewed military attacks with overwhelming numerical superiority, the party leaders not only sought to throw open the gates, but also took every possible step to see that masses of immigrants streamed through them.

This decision on immigration was not the only option, and in some measure it contradicted positions taken in the past. The workers' parties, headed by Mapai, had traditionally advocated selective immigration. Their attitude derived from their conception of the social and economic essence of the state in the making, and their fear lest it be undermined by masses of immigrants unprepared for the task of creating an independent society in a barren land devoid of the appropriate social and productive infrastructure. That was the position taken during the 1920s and 1930s with regard to immigration from Europe, towards immigrants with origins and culture similar to those who had already settled in Palestine to lay the foundations and erect the structures of a new Jewish society. Consequently it was even harder for the leaders of Mapai to decide to fill the land with masses of Jews from Asia and Africa. Although they were largely ignorant about the character of these Jewish communities, they probably anticipated that their absorption would pose problems with which even a well-established and firmly based society would find it difficult to cope. The first years of mass immigration showed that these apprehensions were not illusory: there was imitation, but no real cultural absorption.

The Mapai leaders were not deterred, however, either by the difficulties of cultural absorption or by the economic realities of those years. It was already clear at the onset of mass immigration that Israel lacked jobs as well as a social infrastructure, especially housing, sufficient to absorb so many immigrants: within three years the Jewish population of the state doubled. The imbalance between what was available and what was needed, and the social grievances which they knew would accumulate among the new immigrants as a result of the difficulties of their economic absorption, their poor wages and miserable housing, did not deter the Mapai leaders from deliberately speeding up immigration. They had realised that for Israel's existence — existence and military security being synonymous in Ben-Gurion's vocabulary — the rapid increase in Jewish population was a vital necessity.

In these days of popular sociology, some people argue that the mass immigration was a plot on the part of the veteran residents of the country or, in another version tailored to fit up-to-date polemics, an Ashkenazi ruse. It is claimed that the Ashekenazis (the Jews of European origin and their descendants) asked their leaders to supply them with plenty of hewers of wood and drawers of water, deprived of them as they were by the flight of the Arabs. Mapai, or the veterans, or the Ashkenazis (depending on who is talking) saw the Jews of Africa and Asia as excellent substitutes for the Arabs, actually dual-purpose substitutes, for the immigrants would also supply cannon fodder in future wars against the Arabs. However, not only was there no evidence at the time of this line of argument among the veteran Jewish settlers or their leadership, but the immigrants themselves, especially those who might have seemed destined by nature to be hewers of wood and drawers of water, did not fulfil these expectations. In short, although a brief exposition cannot do full justice to the facts, it can be said that, during the early years of their absorption, the new immigrants put a heavy economic burden upon the veteran community (see Table 1.1). This view is supported by personal memories of those days, and further by the record of the desperate efforts on the part of the government to obtain outside assistance: a loan from the United States, the release of sterling reserves by the British Government, the establishment of an organisation for raising development loans (Israel Bonds), and the like. These efforts were accompanied by the imposition of a stringent rationing system in the country, and by high unemploy-

Table 1.1 Jewish Population 1949–52

	1949	1950	1951	1952
Jewish population (in millions) at the end of the year	1.0	1.2	1.4	1.45
Average Jewish population	0.9	1.1	1.3	1.4
Number seeking work* (in thousands)	6.5	27.9	31.0	25.1

* Those employed in make-work are not included among those seeking employment.

ment, with the unemployed dependent on the state. Later on, David Horowitz, Israel's senior economist at the time, was to recall that there were days when the ability to pay for one more shipload of wheat spelled the difference between continued existence and hunger, pure and simple.

After ten years of stewardship Mapai, or, to use a practically synonymous term, the national leadership, could look back with satisfaction: it had done a good job, measured by the standards generally applied to governments, and particularly to those of developing nations following the ground-rules of democracy. At any rate, that was the judgment of the people: in the elections for the fourth Knesset in 1959, the party, campaigning under the slogan, 'Say "Yes" to the Old Man' (meaning Ben-Gurion), received additional seats.

After it had won 46 seats out of 120 in the elections for the first Knesset (also called the Constituent Assembly), Mapai declined to 40 seats in the third Knesset, elected in 1955. But in the elections for the fourth Knesset in 1959 it rose again to 47 seats, nearly 40 per cent of the house, a record number. This was the prize for past performance, however: during the first decade of Israel's existence two wars were fought and won, a national economy was created virtually from scratch, and the number of immigrants absorbed totalled twice the original population. Had the voters been able to predict the future, the results might have been different. Had the public perceived the wasting erosion of ten years in power scarring Mapai and its leadership, it would have awarded certificates of outstanding achievement to those who had done such great things, but it would have seen that they were no longer fit to rule. The party programme had lost its momentum, and the leadership had failed to renew the national agenda to make it appropriate for the changed conditions prevailing after ten years of Mapai stewardship.

The Lavon Affair

The crisis which exposed the mistake was 'the Lavon Affair'. In May 1960 the General Secretary of the Histadrut, Pinhas Lavon, asked Ben-Gurion to have him cleared from an accusation which had never been made. Six years earlier an inquiry commission, consisting of the President of the Supreme Court, Yitzhak Olshan, and the former Chief of Staff, Yaakov Dori, had found that on the evidence presented to it it could not determine who had ordered a Jewish underground group in Egypt to commit certain acts of sabotage; was it Pinhas Lavon, who was then the Minister of Defence, or was it the chief of military intelligence, Benyamin Guibli? As a result of their own inquiry prior to the establishment of the commission of inquiry, and discussions after the commission had finished its work, the Mapai leadership forced Lavon to resign. Now, in May 1960, he demanded that he be cleared of the allegation that it was he who had ordered the underground network to take actions which led to a tragic outcome. The common explanation for this move is that Lavon calculated that, if he were cleared, he would have a reasonable chance of becoming the candidate for the party leadership and, considering the practically automatic identification between the two, for the premiership if and when Ben-Gurion retired for reasons of age. The latter rejected the request, arguing that since he had not brought the charge against Lavon, he could not exonerate him. Instead, he proposed a judicial inquiry commission as the best way to investigate the matter and rehabilitate Lavon, if that followed from the commission's findings.

Within a few weeks, the controversy between the heads of the two great institutions of Israeli life, the government and the labour federation, the Histadrut, had split public opinion, once more demonstrating the particular status of Mapai in the public mind: the rivals were both Mapai leaders, but an internal party conflict was perceived as a subject of the greatest importance for all the country's citizens. The controversy quickly turned into a total confrontation, gradually assuming the proportions of a civil war within the country's leadership. The struggle paralysed the government and ultimately brought it down, forcing new elections two years before the end of the legal term.

Here one should note that the struggle within Mapai did not have the character of a struggle between two bureaucracies, i.e. the government versus the Histadrut. On the contrary, the split did not follow organisational divisions. In the course of the conflict many party leaders within the government went over from Ben-Gurion's to Lavon's camp. The intramural struggle assumed the characteristics of a systemic crisis, revealing cracks in the regime's foundations. Senior party representatives resorted to strong language, describing their own party's rule as a regime of intimidation and deceit whose leaders were preparing mass graves for each other.

Some years previous to the Lavon Affair, Mapai had been shaken by another controversy which erupted between Prime Minister Ben-Gurion, and the Minister of Foreign Affairs, Moshe Sharett (who had been Prime Minister from 1954 until the elections for the third Knesset in 1955). This controversy did not revolve around the possible responsibility of one of the two men for an action taken long ago, nor yet around their fitness to hold governmental office. Rather it concerned a matter which, at the time, must have seemed vital to all concerned: the question of war and peace, or, more specifically, the proper response to Egypt's closure of the straits of the Red Sea to Israeli shipping and to the threat to internal security posed by Arab infiltrators operating from the territories, and under the protection, of Egypt and Jordan. Ben-Gurion emerged victorious from this controversy, and exploited his victory, among other things, to get rid of Sharett, a well-liked leader who enjoyed considerable support within Mapai. But although the dispute between the two leaders, ending with Sharett's dismissal, had shocked Mapai deeply, it was characterised by great self-restraint, no attempt being made to involve outside factors while it lasted nor after its conclusion.

The difference between the two affairs is conspicuous. On the one hand, a powerful rivalry between two leaders on a subject bearing directly on the security of the country was dealt with by the party without upsetting its leadership or procedures, and, in contrast, a struggle between two leaders of the same party on a subject of a strictly personal nature with which it could not cope on its own, and therefore had to involve both the opposition and the public to determine the outcome.

Various explanations come to mind. One is that Ben-Gurion had grown old and that the time had come to put him out to pasture. Alternatively it is possible to attribute the eruption of the 1960 affair to a public grown sensitive to injustice, whereas in 1956 the discussion took place behind closed doors, masked, among other things, by military censorship. However, Ben-Gurion was no youngster in 1956 either, and it will be recalled how the party actually sought the voters' support with the slogan reminiscent of totalitarian countries: 'Say "Yes" to the Old Man'. And if one examines the other hypothesis mentioned above, one finds that it turns into a question in its own right: why did the party agree to involve the public in the Lavon Affair, and on the initiative of a growing number of its own members, in 1960, and why did it not involve the people at large in 1956, despite the far greater gravity of the question in dispute?

The answer which suggests itself, although it cannot be proved analytically, is that in 1956 the matter in dispute appeared to be the main issue, not the personalities involved in it. Conversely, in 1960 the matter itself was trivial, concerning, as it did, the personal status of the antagonists. The struggle between Ben-Gurion and Sharett befitted a party absorbed in its appointed task, the implementation of a national agenda which was widely agreed upon and acceptable to the loser and his supporters too. Conversely, the struggle between Ben-Gurion and Lavon took place in a party which had achieved its goals and thus no longer had much left to do apart from administering past gains. In brief, in 1956 Mapai was a party in mid-course, on the way towards full implementation of the national agenda. In 1960 it was resting on its laurels with no other goal but to stay in power, bereft of direction and drive.

This is not the place to examine the 1960 affair in detail. Suffice it to note that within a short time it developed into a full-blown scandal, even though the secondary disputants who joined one side or the other made valiant efforts to give it what it lacked: substance sufficient to justify the public uproar. Justice and truth did not depend, despite the claims voiced by Ben-Gurion and his followers, on whether or not a judicial inquiry commission was established to examine what had happened in 1954, or whether Levi Eshkol's manoeuvres (see below) were permissible politics or a subversion of proper procedures. On the opposing side it was argued that acceptance of Ben-Gurion's demands meant the abandonment of democracy and submission to the desire for vengeance or the tyranny of an ageing dictator. However, the moral rosewater with which the two sides so liberally besprinkled themselves could not hide the stink wafting up from the scandal. In 1960 Mapai had basically completed the task of implementing the national agenda it had set for the country, and it was left without a mission or even a sense of one. Only its instinct for power, an essential element in its ability to guide the nation, remained strong, twisting the party into a caricature of itself even in the view of many of its leaders and supporters.

This may serve to explain a phenomenon which had hitherto been unknown in Israel: public alienation from the national leadership, which took the form of widespread hatred of Ben-Gurion, the personal embodiment of Mapai and its rule. The most conspicuous expressions of that alienation were found principally in the academic community, many of whom were Mapai supporters or even activists. Nevertheless, these alienated members of the intelligentsia, who possessed the intellectual capacity and professional knowledge to make out the widening gap between pretensions to office and its actual justification, the ability to formulate a new national agenda, instead became obsessed with the most superficial manifestations of the Lavon Affair. The personal injustice which had allegedly been done to Lavon was placed in the centre of the public stage and became the cynosure of all eyes. It seemed as if Israel's collective intelligence, as represented by the best educated of its professional intelligentsia, had taken an extended leave of absence.

One wonders how it was that, although Mapai had exhausted its programme and its leadership had demonstrated their bankruptcy during the Lavon Affair, the party did not lose power. In fact, in the elections following Ben-Gurion's resignation from the premiership no significant changes took place. The elections for the fifth Knesset in August 1961 did bring a reduction in Mapai's electoral strength from 38.2 to 34.7 per cent; but it remained the leading party, and it formed the government. Mapai's two traditional rivals, the General Zionists and Herut, increased their strength, but not sufficiently to justify an effective claim to form a government of their own.

Here we find a refutation of the general argument that in democracies people vote against the government and not for the opposition. Although the Mapai leaders and the rank and file had jointly done their utmost to reveal the weaknesses and even corruption at the top, no change took place in the line-up for the 1961 elections. The party was saved from the electoral defeat it richly deserved because of the inability of what was known as the bourgeois opposition, Herut and the Liberal Party, to put forward an alternative national agenda and a credible leadership to implement it. It would take another sixteen years before the public drew effective conclusions from what had begun to be evident at the end of the 1950s, namely, that the party whose energy had vitalised the first ten years of independent statehood had shot its bolt, retaining only the practical ability and experience needed for routine administration.

Rise of the Opposition

Since the mid-1950s an internal opposition had been growing within Mapai, centred around the younger party members. These young men demanded appropriate positions of power in the party and its subsidiary organisations, in the government, the Histadrut, and economic organisations: in other words, they launched a personal challenge based principally on the claim that they were more effective and energetic workers. Moreover, towards the climax of the crisis within Mapai, some of the more prominent of the young party members expressed reservations about the party programme itself. These reservations remained fragmentary, however, and a fully worked out alternative to Mapai's traditional national agenda never emerged from these circles. The veteran party members quickly discerned this weakness: in their defensive campaign to preserve their positions of power and the material benefits and social prestige derived from them, they repeatedly asked what substantive reform the pretenders proposed. That question remained without any convincing response.

Moshe Dayan was prominent among the younger men. Endowed with great leadership qualities, a cruel charm, bright, sure of himself, and always iconoclastic, upon his entry into political life in 1958 Dayan launched an attack against the Histadrut and its claim to a quasi-governmental status. Later on, in 1963, having served as Minister of Agriculture in Ben-Gurion's last cabinet and having resigned from that of Levi Eshkol because he had not been promoted to a more important ministry and had also been deprived of influence on defence matters, though he had been Chief of Staff during the Sinai campaign of 1956, he declared:

> Degania, Ain Harod, or Nahalal [among the veteran co-operative agricultural settlements] no longer symbolise the vital centre or the problems of our national existence. Today towns such as Beersheba, Ashdod, or Dimona [the new development towns] are the ones which do.

Dayan's criticism, and the demand for a change in social emphasis, was quickly seized upon by the old guard as a denial of the basic organisational and ideological tenets of Mapai. It derived from an intuitive grasp of the shift that had taken place in the centre of gravity of Israeli society. No longer was Israel the society in which the Histadrut and the co-operative settlements had grown up and been consolidated, and on which the newly established state had depended to provide the foundations of the government and the economy. Now electoral power was concentrated in the cities populated by immigrants, most of whom had no personal memory of the great years of struggle against the British mandate and the supreme efforts invested in establishing, consolidating, and defending the state.

The theoretical distance from Dayan's declaration of 1963 to the Likud election victory in 1977 was a mere step. But Dayan, as happened so often in his eventful career, failed to draw the proper conclusions, perhaps because of his inability to bridge the gap between occasional insights and political synthesis, perhaps because in his heart of hearts he doubted the validity of his own observations, or perhaps because of his unconscious refusal to divorce himself and his political ambitions from the historical elites of Degania and Nahalal from which he had sprung and which he represented to the end of his life. At any rate, neither then, in the late 1950s and early 1960s, nor later did Dayan propose an organised programme in which the rejection of the political claims of the traditional holders of power was complemented by a fully fledged alternative.

Shimon Peres was the other prominent representative of the young guard, and a pioneer of modern industry in Israel. He discerned another aspect of the widening gap between the national agenda identified with Mapai rule and the models for development acceptable to it, on the one hand, and the requirements arising from a national existence in a hostile environment and in a world undergoing swift technological innovation, on the other. At that time Peres was instituting revolutionary technological changes within the closed realm of the defence industry. But, busy as he was at the Ministry of Defence, he also made an ambitious attempt to set out a political platform in a letter sent to Prime Minister Levi Eshkol, in response to his provocative question, 'What do you [young men] really stand for?'

Like Dayan, Peres also placed the development towns at the

centre of his social conception, or, to quote his letter, 'One must raise the development towns . . . to the level of a valued and prized possession of the movement'. This was to be done in the knowledge that 'we are living' in what he called a 'mass society'. The old social elite was weary, according to his analysis, and had turned into an ossified, conservative class. New energy was to be generated by infusing the national elite — i.e., the Labour Movement — with the strength of masses of immigrants living in the development towns. But the party also had to plot a new economic course: yesterday's agriculture and industry could no longer support those employed in them and provide them with a decent living. A new industry had to be developed, that is, an industry which could compete in the modern world. Peres therefore proposed that the party should prepare a national programme, 'Not a departmental, but a movement programme, in which the entire nation will be partners', as he put it. Industrial development would be central to it, and 'modern industry is preferable, embodying the last word in technology'.

However, in political terms, the initiative of Dayan and Peres came too late. In the view of the veteran Mapai leaders, the two younger men merely seemed to be rebelling against the accepted tenets of the movement. The veterans suspected that the promotion of new ideas was merely a cover to disguise the younger leaders' attempt to supplant them either with the aid of modern rhetoric or by simply denying their right to rule as the legitimate heirs of the founding generations. Had Dayan and Peres put forward their ideas immediately after the Sinai campaign of 1956, when the country was caught up in a wave of rapid development, the results might have been different. But the opportunity was missed; Mapai lost the chance to renew its mandate and to provide a vision for the nation, thereby reasserting its claim to another period in power.

During the first half of the 1960s the Israeli public lost its childhood illusions. The 1950s had been years of great creativity: the state was established, about a million immigrants were absorbed, the country's security was maintained by the Israeli Defence Force, which had to prove its mettle in action against infiltrators and during the Sinai campaign. The national economy also expanded sufficiently to support the growing population and showed signs of increasing ability to make use of contemporary technology. Thus the Mapai leadership had implemented the agenda which it had taken up after the War of Independence. Then, in the early 1960s, the machinery started to idle, chiefly propelled by the momentum of its earlier drive. With the removal of Ben-Gurion the leadership became simply an executive, though it is probable that Ben-Gurion's continued presence would have made no difference. His fall did not cause the exhaustion of the national leadership for which he stood; it was rather the result of that exhaustion.

The New-Old Regime

Many people thought that new men in positions of national leadership would be sufficient to consolidate a fresh national agenda and restore the creative drive which had uniquely marked the previous ten years; however, the Eshkol period proved they were mistaken. The public wanted the new team presented by Mapai to succeed: the 1965 elections restored almost all the parliamentary power enjoyed by the party at its peak in 1959. But even sooner than in 1959 the public realised it had struck a bad bargain: the 'new-old' leadership confounded it with the worst economic crisis Israel had known since its establishment.

It is possible to explain the recession of 1966 in Keynesian terms, such as reduction of the government deficit in order to combat inflation, lack of sufficient awareness within the government bureaucracy of the need to forestall unemployment by promoting investment in the infrastructure, and so on. However, the cause lay deeper, namely in the leadership's loss of direction. It proved incapable of providing an appropriate national agenda for the period of calm after a decade of civilian construction and military reinforcement. There was a sense of stagnation accompanied by a loss of faith and a reduction of economic momentum both at the governmental and at the individual level. With a complete lack of public trust and private vigour, unemployment and a spirit of resigned hopelessness spread like wildfire. In a period of worldwide economic expansion, Israel alone was bogged down in a recession: about ten per cent of the work force became unemployed. As a side effect, macabre jokes became widespread, which both expressed the public's pessimism and exacerbated it. Most of them were at the expense of the Prime Minister, Levi Eshkol, although just a year or two before he had been the object of admiration for having freed the country from the tyranny of David Ben-Gurion. The jokes focused on his inability and impotence — mistakenly, as it happens, since he was neither the guilty party nor chief among those responsible for the loss of the dynamism of the 1950s.

The Mapai leadership could not fail to be aware of these public attitudes. Even before the economic crisis, while the party leaders were still busy with the political struggle which culminated in Ben-Gurion's removal from the leadership, they were scanning the horizon for a cure. Since they were firm believers in the power of organisation, they sought an answer to the lack of substance in their programme in the expansion of their organisation. Eshkol's negotiations in 1961 for the purpose of creating a new government, still to be headed by Ben-Gurion, were the start of the acute stage of the crisis which engulfed the veteran leader. During these negotiations Eshkol discovered that Ahdut Haavoda, which had split off from Mapai in 1944 and had combined with Hashomer Hatsair (an even more left-wing party) to form the United Workers Party[1] but had separated from it in 1954, was now prepared to return to the fold and form a permanent partnership with Mapai. There had been signs to this effect even before, particularly since, during the leadership crisis, the leaders of Ahdut Haavoda concentrated their criticism on Ben-Gurion personally. Some of Eshkol's actions between 1961 and 1965, while the groundwork for Ben-Gurion's removal from Mapai was being laid, were guided by his own desire and that of his supporters to create conditions which would allow for the establishment of such a partnership — the New Alignment, as it was then called. The aspirations of Eshkol and his supporters were fulfilled by the broadening of Mapai's institutional basis — its reunification, as it was claimed at the time. The Mapai leaders had long yearned to heal the rift of 1944, and Eshkol's group sought to provide a response both to Ben-Gurion, whose fate was being sealed in the hearts of his comrades, and to the public who felt that the Palestine Workers' Party had ceased to offer a promising vision to the nation.

Did Eshkol and his associates act instinctively in turning to Ahdut Haavoda, or did they do so on the basis of standard practical considerations? The answer to that question does not bear directly on the present inquiry. What is relevant, however, is that by turning, in its hour of need, to Ahdut Haavoda, Mapai blocked the way for the establishment of a coalition with the centre right. Thus, even before the 1965 Knesset elections, the General Zionist Party felt obliged to set up and formalise a partnership with Herut and establish the electoral alliance, Gahal, the basis of today's Likud, which offered an alternative national agenda and eventually captured the government. Therefore, in a sense the tactical moves made by Eshkol and his comrades in the early 1960s paved the way for the political upheaval of 1977. Apparently Eshkol did not see things in terms of a choice between two types of coalition, one on the left and one on the centre-right. He sought rather to create an organisational and quantitative substitute for the lost substance of his own party. In a certain sense — even though by turning to Ahdut Haavoda he was turning leftwards — the step was appropriate; it was a step towards the hard core of the *kibbutzim* affiliated to Ahdut Haavoda to which, for historical reasons, the leaders of Mapai attributed ideological and moral vitality. They had felt the loss of that vitality in their mass party keenly; thus the partnership was intended to help Mapai not only by increasing its numbers but also by developing a new political message. Nevertheless, it was still a strange move: in order to give substance to a party of the 1960s, Eshkol sought the help of those who had provided it during the 1920s and 1930s.

A Definition of Mapai

At this point a brief digression is appropriate in order to classify the national agenda associated with Mapai in political science terms. Since Mapai defined itself as a socialist-Zionist party, it is generally assumed that the party was what it said it was: Zionist in its striving for a sovereign Jewish state, socialist as to the internal arrangements of that state. However, upon closer examination, this conclusion appears at least partly doubtful.

It should be noted that during the 1950s the term 'Zionism' was synonymous with empty, pointless rhetoric. This derisory use of the term grew from general experience. Although the first tenet in the Zionist credo was the desire to immigrate to the Land of Israel of one's own free will, only a minority of those who actually came to the country after the establishment of the state were Zionists in that sense. Some were displaced persons who in fact had nowhere else to go; others were uprooted from their countries of origin and brought to Israel because of a decision made by the Israeli Government. Neither group immigrated of its own free will; they were brought to Israel because other people, who had already implemented their own Zionist beliefs, wanted them to come. Thus the power and effectiveness of the Zionist element of voluntary immigration in the ideological armoury of Mapai seemed dubious during the 1950s, especially when one recalls that, in the minds of the leadership, bringing Jews to Israel was at least partly a response to the need to fill the empty spaces left by the mass exodus of the Arabs during the War of Independence.

As for Mapai's socialism, that may be judged by the results of its stewardship during the first decade of the state. Certainly the number of so-called socialist islands among the agricultural settlements increased greatly, as did their population and their economic power. At the same time, the Histadrut enterprises such as Koor (an industrial investment and management group), Solel Boneh (a construction company), and Hamashbir Hamerkazi (a chain of retail and wholesale distributors) also grew in strength. However, at the end of the period, principally owing to the activities of Pinhas Sapir, who had been made responsible for industrial development in 1955, the scope of private enterprise was substantially broadened. Moreover, this did not simply happen: the party advocated a mixed economy, and when Sapir recognised that the private sector was missing, he endeavoured to create it, principally by using government funds which were distributed freely.

Socialists normally distinguish between the need for establishing welfare institutions such as the Histadrut Sick Fund or the National Insurance Institute, on the one hand, and the deliberate redistribution of national income by the government to secure social equality, on the other. Similarly, they accept the distinction between the struggle for increased income and improved working conditions as a goal in itself and the process known as the class struggle, the purpose of which is to prepare the ground for the social control (either governmental or co-operative) of the means of production. On May Day, 1949 Golda Meir proclaimed that her party aspired to 'Socialism in our time', and she was certainly referring to something other than the mixed economy and the social welfare institutions which then existed. But in fact Mapai did very little to change the character of the economic regime for the benefit of the workers, apart from giving them political control over certain capital resources. At the end of the 1950s and in the early 1960s a profit-oriented entrepreneurial class began to emerge, professing managerial norms, and this took place under the auspices of governments led by Mapai, and even with their explicit encouragement.

Therefore, if one is to judge from behaviour and the intended effects resulting from it, one can define the national agenda which guided Mapai's actions during the first decade of the state not as Zionist-socialist but rather as settler-statist. To the extent that there was a difference between self-definition and actual behaviour, it did not appear to concern either the party or its leadership. Everyone was too busy with high priority activity to bother with precise self-definition.

The tension between the aspirations of the practical members of Mapai, who sought a cure for their party's loss of direction and the crumbling of its organisational structures, and the yearnings of the Labour intelligentsia for the rekindling of ancient inspiration, is clearly set out in a long article by Yitzhak Ben-Aharon, 'Change Before Disaster Strikes', published in *Lamerhav* in January 1963. The author points out that there had been far-reaching ideological agreement among the workers' parties, but that they had been over loyal to existing institutions; 'First the substance gave rise to a framework, but now the framework has outlived the substance'. In practical political terms, this was a positive response to the quest of the Mapai leadership to breathe new life into a regime which had already accomplished the better part of its own platform, and to restore its power by strengthening it organisationally. Moreover, Ben-Aharon suggested that the mere joining of Mapai and Ahdut Haavoda in the New Alignment would be insufficient, and he demanded that Mapam, the United Workers' Party,[2] be included as well, thus calling for the 'reunification' of the labour movement. To those who asked how that would be possible in view of the chronic differences of opinion, the long history of controversies over principles, and the organisational rivalries among the prospective partners, he responded not only by denying the importance of separate organisations, but also with a colourful definition of substantive issues: 'Our homes are full of carrion and broken crockery, and that refuse smothers our spiritual life'.

In Ben-Aharon's opinion, the government headed by Mapai, but which included members of Ahdut-Haavoda and Mapam, had not carried out a socialist national agenda. The social institutions which grew up under Mapai rule, products of a working-class background, were left over from the pre-state period: the *kibbutzim* and co-operative agricultural settlements in general, the Sick Fund, and the business enterprises owned by the Histadrut. What was created after the founding of the state had not prevented social and economic corruption and had perhaps even hastened the process. Ben-Aharon did not couch his criticism in Marxist terms, nor did he make use of the sociological terminology current in public discussions during the period of the Mandate and the first decade of the state, such as 'statism', and 'colonising regime', to define the character of the national agenda. However, his opinion of the substance of that agenda was implicit in what he advocated to replace it and in what he prescribed for the reformed Labour movement. This was an agenda which could properly be termed socialist, and the author summed it up as follows: freezing the income of half the population; immediately raising the income of the poorest quarter of the population; and reducing the income of the quarter of the population with the largest share of the national income.

The socialism implicit in this national agenda exhibited two main features: the use of the state authority available to the reformed Labour Party in order to implement it; and its pronounced redistributive character — class struggle would be conducted by the government for the purpose of improving the lot of the poorest quarter of the population. Eight of the sixteen clauses proposed by Ben-Aharon were thoroughly redistributive in character, and on the basis of this national agenda he predicted 'enormous, renewed impetus to ensure the creative and pioneering character of the economy and the state'.

The arguments put forward in its favour are the most interesting feature of the proposed redistributive programme. In Ben-Aharon's article there is no shortage of expressions of hostility towards the rich and those who profit at the expense of their fellow citizens, especially those who get rich on public funds, but one finds precious little evidence of the author's awareness of social exploitation in the Marxist sense, or of sympathy with the weak and the oppressed. Nor is his major proposition framed in socialist class terms. It is actually state-oriented, focusing on the necessity of freeing Israel from dependence on foreign aid, which, in Ben-Aharon's opinion, has distorted Israeli society by causing it to lose its pioneering character. This argument appears in the very first clause of his programme of action, where he writes: 'At the end of the first half of the ten year plan, no more foreign aid or assistance to improve the standard of living of the Israeli population will be requested. Israel will have a positive balance of trade, [excluding] long range investment in development and defense.' The purport is clear: 'The net deficit . . . will be decreased annually by increasing exports, and whatever is not obtained through exports will have to come out of consumption and personal services and from government administration'. In conclusion, for such a programme to be implemented, Ben-Aharon argues that 'it must bear the stamp of severity, of austerity, of limited consumption, and of living by our own efforts'.

Thus the message of Ben-Aharon's essay was first that he approved of the efforts invested by the Mapai leadership in enlarging the organisation under its control by grafting onto it another party or parties, its neighbours on the political map. Second, he also grasped what Eshkol and his friends had not, namely that an enlarged organisation would not necessarily attract more electoral support. For an expanded party to maintain itself in office, it would have to offer a new national agenda to the electorate in place of the one which was no longer attractive because it had essentially been implemented already and the social thrust of which had exhausted itself along the road from the *Yishuv* to the state. Ben-Aharon was certainly aware that at that time Mapai and the other labour parties under its wing were undergoing a crisis of depletion. That crisis was not, essentially, a personal one afflicting only the Mapai leadership, but rather a party crisis, or, if you will, the crisis of an entire political movement which no longer had a rationale for holding power.

The answer which Ben-Aharon offered to this basic problem may be described as an injection of positive socialism into the state. The state, activated by immigration and the construction of a broadly based economic infrastructure and productive superstructures during its first ten years, was now called upon to concentrate its efforts on two goals which had been neglected or ignored: a radical redistribution of national income and wealth, and a freeing of the economy from dependence on foreign aid, at least for current consumption. In proposing these two goals, Ben-Aharon married state sovereignty with redistributive social policy, both of which were meant to restore the drive to the ruling parties which adopted them.

Only Ben-Aharon's organisational proposals were found acceptable. At the end of a process marked by many sudden reversals and crises, the labour movement was united. However, his substantive proposals, which were intended to satisfy the needs of a large portion of the population, were rejected. The social dynamic tended towards an increasingly bourgeois way of life, harvesting the fruits of one's labours: the idea that after ten years of strenuous effort and war — not to mention the Holocaust in Europe and the social catastrophe of mass immigration — people would have to face another decade of 'severity, austerity, and limited consumption' was unacceptable. When a party emerged whose principal social message was that the right moment had finally come, Ben-Aharon's pessimistic forecast materialised, for as he had foreseen a religious right-wing coalition was lurking outside the gates.

Ethnic Discrimination

In order to understand the Israeli political process, it is important to note that aside from a single exceptional instance, the problems and issues of immigration and of immigrant groups have not, in fact, been a central issue in the political struggle at the party level.

These words were written by Professor Shmuel Eisenstadt in his book, *Israeli Society, Background, Development, and Problems,*[3] the second Hebrew edition of which appeared in 1973. The book covers its subject up to 1965, and when it was first published, Eisenstadt, one of Israel's most prominent sociologists, had no reason to fear that his students and colleagues at the Hebrew University would challenge his conclusion. This was still the case when the second edition was published, six years later. However, it is doubtful whether today, looking back from our present vantage point, the author would be tempted to write as he did, although in point of fact his words were true of the period to which they referred. Today absorption and ethnic origins are matters of great concern both to the public and to the government, and they are the focus of the political debate. During the 1950s and the early 1960s this was not the case, and it is noteworthy that in the catalogue of social problems presented in Ben-Aharon's article, the question of ethnic groups, or, to use the rather tired slogan, 'ethnic discrimination', does not appear at all.

The 'exceptional instance' mentioned in Professor Eisenstadt's book took place in mid July 1959, and the timing, five months before the elections to the Knesset, clearly helped to veil the message which emerges from it. A resident of a Haifa neighbourhood known as Wadi Salib, described afterwards as a

well-known drunkard, caused a disturbance and was wounded by
the policemen who came to arrest him. About a third of the
residents of that poor neighbourhood — afterwards the newspapers
reported that living conditions there were not among the worst in
the country — had been immigrants from North Africa. A number
of them then formed a group which staged a riot in Hadar
Hacarmel, a more affluent neighbourhood, during which store-
windows were broken and automobiles turned over and burned. In
short, they staged an early version of the violent demonstration, a
phenomenon which subsequently became a not particularly
shocking news item in Israel. In the following few days, reporters
discovered that a group calling itself the 'Union of North African
Immigrants' was behind the riot, which goes to show that while the
event was perhaps not typical, it had also not been a spontaneous
outburst of rage on the part of unfortunate individuals seeking the
attention of the people of Haifa.

Within a short time the government appointed a commission to
investigate the matter. However, the commission did not deal with
the general aspects of the event — real or imagined ethnic discrimination against Oriental immigrants — but instead limited itself to
investigating the sequence of events in Haifa and the specific causes
of the riot. At that time Israel had not yet been overrun by
sociologists, and the public was therefore insufficiently aware of the
need to examine social events in depth. Nevertheless in this case
there were two good reasons for paying heed to the event: this was
the first time that a group of immigrants defined itself on the basis of
its origins and adopted the method of the violent demonstration to
protest against discrimination, although the experiences it had
undergone and which drove its members to adopt that method were
not substantially different from those undergone by other groups of
immigrants. All the immigrants, without exception, had experienced alienation and humiliation and encountered discrimination
which impeded their promotion at work and sometimes even
deprived them of a livelihood. However, no other group resorted to
demonstrations of any kind, let alone violent ones. The second
reason why the event merited attention lay in the manner in which
the demonstration was justified; that was unique in its time. It
displayed a profound hatred which even the most lenient and
forgiving interpretation could not possibly reconcile with the
standard, idyllic view of the return to Zion and of brethren dwelling
together in peace.

In this context it is worth quoting in full a letter to the editor of the daily newspaper *Haaretz*:

> I wish to comment on Mr Yehoshua Gilboa's report in *Haaretz* of July 12, 'The Broken Windows on Hadar Hacarmel'. According to him, they 'must serve as a warning'.
>
> Of what? What warning? What are you warning against? Is it against our discriminatory rulers? Or is it against those who are discriminated against and oppressed? Why is it that you happened to recall just now that Oriental Jews, who did not grow up under democratic rule, pose a threat to your democracy?
>
> In fact Oriental Jews are 65 per cent of the inhabitants of this country and their legal and historical right is no less and in fact even greater than yours, to live in it with equal rights, not only obligations. Despite your preposterous claims and contemptible accusations regarding their ignorance and democratic immaturity and your propaganda against their loyalty, Oriental Jews administered states and governments in both the distant and recent past in their many countries of origin. They were not slaves, as you described them and still picture them to yourselves.
>
> Please tell all the young police officers to whom you spoke that they have no right to complain because they are not permitted to use the Nazi methods of repression which they learned from their experience of persecution in the recent past. Let the hand wither that is raised against the Oriental Jews to silence them or prevent them from demanding their elementary rights of equality and inclusion in the life of the state.
>
> It is the moral and formal duty of the Minister of the Police and the Commissioner, Mr Nachmias, themselves Oriental Jews, to bring disciplinary action against those loose-lipped officers who claimed that 'Oriental Jews only respect force!' Otherwise I shall deny their authority and leadership over their men.
>
> How you revile us! Until when will you revile us? Why do you continue to protect a police sergeant who shot a drunken man? Is it because he is western, a member of the master race?
>
> As for Almogi [the local labour boss] and his storm troopers operating from his Hadar, if a group of Oriental Jews is ever attacked, I and many tens of thousands like myself, will surely come, even if I have to sacrifice my life in that war, for it is a war of life and death for us and our children, to bring an end to their

suffering from your discrimination, of which we have had
enough.

The letter speaks for itself, and all comment is superfluous except to
point out that no other controversial public event — and there was
no scarcity of them in a country which, at that time also, tended to
get highly excited about matters great and small — provoked a
reaction so deeply fraught with anger and hatred.

After several weeks of discussion, the explosive issues raised by
the Wadi Salib riots were carefully wrapped up and placed on the
shelf. The public, led by its politicians, preferred to believe they
were dealing with a marginal group whose problems could be solved
in the normal political manner, by improving local conditions and
by giving jobs to some of the members of the community claiming to
have suffered discrimination. The traces left by the event were faint,
although those who sought the meaning of the events of Wadi Salib
in their social context might have looked for it in Moshe Dayan's
remark, quoted above, concerning the transfer of Israel's vital
centres from Degania and Nahalal to the immigrant towns of
Beersheba and Ashdod. However, Dayan's words aroused only
irritation: the public and its leaders did not wish to know.

The first decade in the history of renewed Jewish statehood began
with a bloody war. In the middle of that decade a second war was
fought in which, for the first time, two basic tenets of the defence
doctrine developed by the IDF and ratified by the government, that
is, by the Prime Minister, David Ben-Gurion, were applied: the pre-
emptive strike and carrying the war deep into enemy territory. Two
wars in ten years ought to have made it clear that not only was the
problem of Israel's relations with its neighbours still unsolved, but
also that it was still at an acute stage. But the subject attracted
relatively little public attention in comparison with the intensive and
even obsessive treatment it receives today. Even though the death
and destruction wrought by the terrorists, the fedayeen, as they
styled themselves, were extensively reported in the media, the
broader questions arising from them were not included in the
discussion of the national agenda. Ben-Aharon, for example,
reviewed all the major topics that then concerned the labour
movement and especially Mapai, the leading party, and the
government it led, but he did not include the Israel-Arab conflict.
Similarly Professor Eisenstadt's book, which presented a detailed
review of the topics agitating the political community during the

first fifteen years of the state, failed to mention that the state was still bounded by cease-fire lines, in other words, had no recognised international boundaries, and that its relations with its neighbours were a moot issue calling for some solution. Nor did the two authors, although knowledgable men in touch with the situation in the country, discuss the enmity of the Arab countries or the steps which ought to be taken to resolve the conflict. In retrospect it seems that the conflict with the neighbouring countries was perceived by the public and by the political community as a sort of fact of nature: like the sun rising in the east or the passage of the seasons. Means and methods of dealing with Israeli-Arab relations were simply absent from the national agenda.

A fascinating consequence of this state of affairs was the fact that the war against Egypt in 1956, which Israel fought as part of an international coalition, came and went without leaving any political trace. After an impressive military victory there came a superficially disappointing political conclusion — only superficially disappointing, in that as a result of the war the borders remained quiet for nearly ten years, a decade which later turned out to have been the golden age of the reconstituted Jewish commonwealth. The government was not called to account for its apparent failure; in this the difference between the reaction of the public and the political establishment to the outcome of the Sinai Campaign and what took place following Operation Peace for the Galilee, two wars which have a good deal in common, is highly instructive. During the first period people were barely conscious of the Arab-Israeli dispute as something attributable to men, whereas in the second period that awareness was a central subject of public discussion.

Inasmuch as the enmity of the Arabs and its most virulent manifestation, war, was not viewed as a phenomenon belonging to the realm of politics, but rather as a kind of fact of nature, no systematic and sustained effort was made to discover its causes; nor were the possible ways of reducing it discussed. Nor, conversely, did any leader even consider the possibility of using military force to break the Arabs' will to destroy Israel. This possibility served as a fundamental tenet in David Ben-Gurion's thinking, evidence of his harsh realism. But he did not hold with the opinion adopted later by others that a decisive military victory was possible.

In other words, during the first decade there was no analytical discussion of relations with Israel's neighbours of the kind so well known today. The settling of the Arab-Israel conflict was not included in the national agenda, nor did it serve as a topic of debate between the opposing camps, nor had it yet been deemed worthy of academic investigation. The standard bearers of nationalist radicalism, too, ignored Israeli-Arab relations. The Herut Movement was preoccupied by relations with Germany, inflation, and the decisive influence of the Histadrut bureaucracy in society, and the slogan of 'Both Banks of the Jordan' was effectively ignored. This was a time of glory for Dr Yohanan Bader, the Herut spokesman on economic and social affairs. Menachem Begin and his comrades, the former Irgun Zevai Leumi commanders, did not yet set the political tone of their party.

At that time Israel tended to regard the issue of relations with its Arab neighbours in the same way as the Dutch regard the sea: without reflection or discussion, the public agreed to invest its best efforts and resources in building dams against the tide which was liable to rise all of a sudden, without any cause accessible to human reason. The IDF, created at the height of the War of Independence, was equipped with the best weaponry that the new state could afford. For its part, the general staff invested an impressive intellectual effort in the development of a doctrine of warfare and of force structure based on a rational analysis of the conflict and the resources available to deal with it. As General Yisrael Tal wrote in the journal *Maarakhot* in 1975, the main points of that doctrine were:

> The IDF must defend the Jewish state in its given territory: it must carry out its task in awareness of the quantitative relations between the two sides (few against many); and it must be aware of the basic assymetry that informs its operations: if the Arabs defeat Israel, that will be the end of the state; but no IDF victory on the battlefield, even if decisive, will destroy even a single Arab state.

One operational conclusion based on these fundamentals of military doctrine was that the IDF had to seek victory on the battlefield by relying on armour and the air force. The seizure of territory in the wake of a military victory was meant to provide the political leadership with a bargaining counter with which to buy respite from the Arab campaign aimed at the destruction of Israel, or, alternatively, to acquire a position of strategic superiority to be exploited until the cease-fire.

It follows that the IDF was regarded by the political leadership as a tool — whether or not it was jointly used with other political tools — for maintaining security by military means. As for normalising relations with the Arabs, that was seen as beyond Israel's grasp. They would be normalised as a result of decisions to be made, if they were made, elsewhere. Paradoxically, this political view, shared by many (although there were those who disagreed, and who, for that reason, were relegated to the sidelines), lacked a political character. To return to the analogy of the Dutch and the sea, war was seen as a natural element which could not be controlled, although a defence had to be found against its violence. Just as there is no need to discuss the need to build dikes, and their construction should naturally be left to professionals, so the Israeli Government entrusted the dangerous issue of friction with its neighbours to the professionals on the general staff. In effect, the public, its political representatives, and its leaders were denying the famous saying of von Clausewitz, that war is an extension of politics by other means. In any event, that is what is indicated by the absence of any substantive discussion of the relations between Israel and its neighbours, of the possibility of influencing them in any deliberate way, or of policies to be adopted for that purpose. The issue of relations with the Arabs simply did not figure in the public debate, and consequently, it was also absent from the national agenda.

Notes

1. Ahdut Haavoda split from Mapai in 1944 for several reasons, the chief of them being its opposition to the partition of Palestine advocated by Ben-Gurion as the only practicable means of achieving a Jewish State. Hazhomer Hatsair, a political party even further to the left than Ahdut Haavoda, had for many years advocated co-operation with the Arab inhabitants and the establishment of a bi-national state in Palestine.

2. Mapam (the Hebrew initials for United Workers' Party) was the result of the combination of Ahdut Haavoda and Hashomer Hatzair before the establishment of the State of Israel. When the two parties split in 1954 Hashomer Hatzair retained the name of the United Workers' Party.

3. Shmuel N. Eisenstadt, *Israeli Society, Background, Development and Problems*, (Magnes Publications, Jerusalem, 1967).

2 SALVATION IN BLOOD AND FIRE

A State of Unpreparedness

The least planned war is what Moshe Dayan called the Six Day War in his autobiography, *Milestones*.[1] It came upon the country's leadership and its citizens with breathtaking suddenness, from an unexpected direction, and with an unprecedented fury that left both participants and observers stunned. Events came to a head, a crisis blew up, took on existential proportions, and was dissipated with lightning speed: all this in less than a month from start to finish. The tempest shook the country, giving its leaders no respite to orient themselves, wrenching them out of one historical era and flinging them into the next.

As we noted earlier, the national agenda with which the new state had set out on its way had been more or less accomplished by the end of the first decade. Since the early 1960s society was merely free-wheeling with one political uproar following on the heels of another. In 1966, about a year and a half before the events to be discussed now, the economy also collapsed: the public faced a recession that destroyed its belief in unlimited growth. Simultaneous with these political and economic shocks, signs of shakiness appeared in the external stability of the situation, putting in jeopardy one of the prime achievements of the Sinai Campaign of 1956.

People had high hopes of Levi Eshkol and the government he formed in 1965. The foundations were being laid for a new sort of bond with the United States; for the first time it had agreed to supply Israel with advanced weaponry. And the Prime Minister and his Foreign Minister Abba Eban, began to speak of a new era of understanding with the Soviet-oriented Arab states, with the help of the Soviet Union. Talk about the 'Spirit of Tashkent' filled the air (referring to the successful mediation between India and Pakistan accomplished by the Soviet Premier, Aleksei Kosygin, in the Uzbek city of Tashkent). The desire to settle Israel's external problems, and the hope that what men of good will desire would come about, inspired Eshkol and the society which he both represented and symbolised at that time.

However, things did not turn out as hoped. From 1964 on, a series of skirmishes took place between the IDF and the Syrian army in the north, focused on the Jordan River tributaries, the Banyas and the Hatsbani. Israel sought to divert its share of the water, as allocated under the internationally agreed Johnston plan[2] for its division, to the national water carrier. The Syrians also claimed the water. Heavy weapons were brought to the front. IDF tanks fired on Syrian bulldozers as they worked to divert the streams. The tension on the northern border increased. The Syrians used their artillery against Israeli settlements in the Galilee, and the IDF attacked from the air. At the peak of the confrontation six Syrian planes were shot down near Damascus. Following the logic of the situation, most Israelis believed that if there was to be a war, it would break out in the north.

A surprise was in store for them: the crisis did not come on the northern border but in the south, and it was not provoked by a local matter like the use of the Jordan waters. The Egyptian President, Gamal Abdul Nasser, defined the conflict in unequivocal terms: on 26 May 1967 he told a delegation of Arab trade unionists that, if Israel took aggressive action against Egypt or Syria, 'the war against Israel will be total, and its goal will be the destruction of Israel'. In view of the steps he took, moving the Egyptian army into Sinai, closing the Straits of Tiran, and demanding the removal of the UN forces which occupied Sharm Al-Sheikh and patrolled the border of the Gaza Strip, there could be no doubt of his seriousness: within less than two weeks the State of Israel was confronted with a threat to its very existence.

From the middle of May 1967 until the end of the month the Israeli Government seemed to be under a malign spell. Although the closure of the Straits of Tiran was a *casus belli*, Israel did not respond to the Egyptian provocation by opening the straits by force. Instead it became involved in hopeless diplomatic manoeuvres. The IDF pressed the government to call up the reserves, and when the authorisation was given, it converted itself in short order to a battle-ready military machine — in sharp contrast to its civilian masters, who vacillated between various explanations of what was happening along the borders. The IDF was given a free hand to prepare for war, using that freedom efficiently despite the temporary nervous collapse which took the chief of Staff, Yitshak Rabin, out of action between 23 and 25 May. In fact, the IDF acted in the way Israeli society had been functioning since the beginning of the decade, without a master plan, driven by the life instinct and the momentum of events, but with no direction. During at least the first stages of the crisis the military command had not yet set a war aim for the IDF in the event of the government ordering it to open fire. Things were even less clear within the government.

The bewilderment of the political leadership revealed itself in its inability to determine the nature of the Egyptian challenge: was it an exercise in intimidation intended as a conditional warning ('If you attack Syria, we shall attack you'), or had President Nasser made a firm decision to bring about Israel's downfall either by psychological warfare or on the battlefield? The inability early in the crisis to understand that the country's existence was being threatened — although within a few days it became clear to all that such was the nature of the threat — was a further consequence of the confusion and lack of direction which had characterised the political leadership in the first half of the 1960s. This confusion had led to self-delusion, to belief in the magical effect of moral 'values', and to the expectation that the Soviet Union and the Arabs would collaborate in resolving the Arab-Israeli conflict. In these circumstances the IDF's effectiveness was limited to the area of its technical responsibility. It could call up the reserves, and it could press the political leaders to respond to the Egyptian challenge with massive force, in no small measure in response to pressures from the mobilised soldiers and based on the realisation that a reserve army could not remain on top alert for ever. However, confusion also gripped the army, but a different sort of confusion: the IDF had difficulty in identifying the strategic goals of the war. As is common in such cases, the command preferred to act cautiously: it planned to drive the Egyptian army back from the borders and seize something of military value — an area including the Gaza Strip and western Sinai as far as El Arish — so that the politicians would be able to bargain afterwards, giving back the territories, it was hoped, in return for reopening the Straits of Tiran.

Throughout history it has been customary to name a period after a prominent ruler: between the Six Day War and the Yom Kippur War Moshe Dayan became the eponymous leader of Israel. Perhaps his meteoric rise during the time of paralysis in the second half of May was possible because he was outside the mainstream of Israeli politics, isolated and disappointed, but also free from the confusion that gripped the public and its leaders. On 22 May Dayan came out in rather general terms for a military confrontation with Egypt.

Within 24 hours he managed to sharpen his insight into the situation: he called for an attack against Egypt 'hitting them hard and destroying hundreds of tanks and planes'. Given the logic of his advice, although he did not say so explicitly, Egypt, with its army mostly destroyed, would be forced, willy-nilly, to concede Israel's right to use the straits. However, logic is not the same as a comprehensive view of the problem and the means for solving it; hence his principal reservation about the way the government was dealing with the crisis. As he wrote in the diary he began to keep at the time:

> I did not hear [during a meeting between the leaders of the government and the opposition in the presence of the Chief of Staff and his assistant] of any general plan, either political or military, for the war: nor did I hear of any link between the military campaign and the opening of the straits.

The problem of the straits solved itself later, after the government had been pushed into war by the force of circumstances, after Dayan had been appointed Minister of Defence, and after the Egyptian army had been destroyed in eastern Sinai according to the revised plan of operations. The IDF victory brought about the reopening of the straits more or less as an afterthought. As for a combined military and political plan of action, in retrospect one can discern a combination of political actions which proved to have facilitated the opening of hostilities. Later on some people praised the wisdom of the delaying tactic with which they credited the government. However, the delay in opening fire was not deliberate but rather the result of hesitation about taking irrevocable action. The government failed to act because it did not understand the situation, and once it grasped the seriousness of the crisis, it was still incapable of decision. In fact, a tie vote on whether to go to war at one of the cabinet meetings was among the factors leading to Eshkol's removal from the defence ministry.

In retrospect, the events of the last two weeks of May look like the race between the tortoise and the hare: Nasser dissipated all his energy at the outset and had no strength left for the ultimate effort of attacking Israel, whereas the Israeli tortoise managed to muster its forces for a final sprint at the end of the race. But Israel went to war with no intentions beyond breaking out of the Arab stranglehold. When the IDF stood at the cease-fire lines on 10 June, the Straits of Tiran were open and the Arab armies defeated, but Israel had no idea what to do with its victory. The problem that had grown into an existential crisis of the sort just described was a political one, which neither the war nor the total military victory brought any nearer to a solution. Nor did the Israeli Government have any blueprint for its solution.

At that time a good deal of attention was certainly given to the unchanging political realities: the public and the leadership continued to regard the stubborn hostility of the Arab states in the way one regards a natural phenomenon. At any rate, the resolutions of the Arab summit meeting at Khartoum — no peace, no negotiations, and no recognition — hardly surprised anyone. They also saddened very few people, if any. Public life, which had been devoid of values and directionless since the beginning of the decade, was now saturated with the victory, the way it had been obtained and the territorial fruits it had borne. The war, its achievements, and the challenges it posed, far exceeding anything previously faced by the Israeli public and its leaders, provided the ingredients for a new national agenda.

The Exaltation of Victory

Once the battle was over, the vacuum began to be filled with an almost obsessive concern with the war itself, its heroes, its commanders, and its weaponry. A feverish inquiry into the details of the battles began: the acts of heroism, the biographies of the commanders, and the technological marvels of the aircraft and tanks. The country was flooded with picture books about the war. Israelis also began to sing their own praises: the self-congratulatory speech of the Chief of Staff on the liberated campus of the Hebrew University on Mount Scopus is highly representative of the picture book era. The nation had been saved from a threat to its existence, and in this way it expressed its gratitude for the salvation brought to it by its army. It is noteworthy, however, that the political leadership, though by law and custom responsible for the army, received no share of the praise. The only member of the government who did receive praise was the stranger in its midst, Moshe Dayan, mainly because of his military background and his position as Minister of Defence directly in charge of the army. Later, attempts were made to minimise his part in the victory, but whether or not the critics were correct, they had no effect on his public position or his political power, which was based on his popularity with the general public.

Why was the victory in the Six Day War not attributed to the political leadership as it had been in the two previous wars? In 1948 the names of Yigael Yadin and Yigael Allon, the outstanding commanders of the IDF at the time, were also on everyone's lips, as was that of Moshe Dayan, when, as Chief of Staff, the forces under his command achieved a military victory in 1956. But people then saw David Ben-Gurion as the leader, and they regarded the generals as technicians merely assisting the Prime Minister, to whom the victor's crown rightfully belonged.

The reason for the difference seems to be that the two previous wars were viewed as secondary incidents in the main story of the establishment of the state in 1948 and its continued construction and reinforcement afterwards. Conversely, in 1967 the public was preoccupied with an economic crisis and a crisis in the political leadership. One sign of the political crisis was the fact that, a few days before the first shot was fired, Levi Eshkol, the man at the pinnacle of the political pyramid, was forced to give up the defence portfolio, and to include Dayan, as well as Menachem Begin and Yosef Sapir of Gahal, in his government of national unity. People had lost faith not just in one man's ability to act, but in the entire government. Its loss of direction was a clear consequence of the loss of the very capacity to frame a national agenda acceptable to the public which had incapacitated Mapai since early on in the second decade of the state's existence. This incapacity eroded its self-confidence and impaired its ability to function independently, without recourse to outside assistance. The phenomenon which was first apparent during the Lavon Affair recurred: unlike its self-sufficiency in the Sharett crisis, to fight the war Mapai needed reinforcements from outside its ranks in order to overcome the weakness afflicting its leadership. And all this took place in full view of the public. People could not fail to sense that the claim to political leadership was hollow; for this reason it was not accorded the praise due to the victor.

As the war and those who had fought it came to monopolise public attention, Israelis flooded into the recently liberated territories: Sinai, Sharm Al-Sheikh, the Golan, and especially Jerusalem and the landscape of the West Bank attracted masses of tourists. Whether he wished to feast his eyes on the historical sites of the land of his fathers, to view the Hula Valley spread out beneath him, to lose himself in the Sinai desert, or simply to buy a basket or some cheap glassware from Arabs in Samaria or Hebron or to see white flags flapping in recently captured villages, the average Israeli threw himself into the occupied territories as if seized by benign madness. The abstract concept of the homeland thus acquired concrete meaning: the land and the scriptural place names revitalised the Bible, and the Bible sanctioned the renewed possession of the land. Pictures of paratroopers with tears in their eyes as they stood on the Temple Mount, or of the sceptic, not to say latter-day pagan, Moshe Dayan, pushing a petition into a crack in the Western Wall as if he were an old-fashioned, orthodox Jew, left an ineradicable impression on the public mind. Thus the expansion of the country's borders and the reunification of the ancient homeland provided legitimisation, half religious, half historical, for a new national agenda.

In retrospect, the hesitancy of the political leadership to adapt itself to the new attitudes which were increasingly taking hold of the public is rather surprising. True, at one of the first post-war cabinet meetings the government set up a planning group to think about what should be done now that the war was over; it did not accomplish much, however. Even more striking from today's point of view was the evident lack of interest in Judea and Samaria. Why was their future never seriously considered during those crucial weeks? Admittedly, the Egyptian challenge dominated the picture, even after Jordan joined the Arab coalition against Israel on 30 May. The Israeli government went far beyond what can be termed lack of interest however: it appealed to King Hussein on the morning of 5 June, asking him not to open hostilities, and promising that Israel, for its part, would honour the *status quo*; in other words, it gave up its claim to reunify the country in advance. One might argue that, even if Hussein had agreed, an Israeli victory over Egypt and Syria would have created a new situation on the eastern border as well. However, even if Israel had achieved decisive military superiority on the eastern border, it still could have done little more than press for minor changes here and there in Jerusalem and perhaps near Latrun — a salient astride the Tel Aviv-Jerusalem axis. In June of 1967 Israel and the international community still maintained relations of mutual respect with each other, and the international community would not have countenanced a flagrant violation of the territorial *status quo* between Israel and Jordan. Moshe Dayan himself, who was later to raise the banner of the Land of Israel, whether in its historical or its archaeological guise, commented at the time: 'We did not go to war to conquer the West Bank'.

Concerning Jerusalem alone there was no doubt. Within a few days East Jerusalem was annexed. A law enacted in the Knesset on 28 June established the municipal boundaries within which Israeli law applied, and, in addition, the symbolic action was taken of removing the physical barriers which had divided the city for twenty years. Against the background of these two decisive actions the government's hesitancy and ambivalence with regard to the other parts of the land of Israel are even more conspicuous. On the night of 10 June, Dayan told a journalist that he was waiting for a telephone call from King Hussein. In other words, he expected an initiative for negotiations which would settle the future of the land of Israel. A few days afterwards the government proposed a settlement with the Arab countries on the basis of the mandatory boundaries, that is, recognising the Jordan River as Israel's eastern border. Three months later, however, in September, Dayan told a reporter of the London *Sunday Times* that he was prepared to return the West Bank to Hussein if the latter would agree to its demilitarisation. The statement was afterwards denied, though not by Dayan himself, and in such a way as to indicate that the journalist had in fact reported his remarks accurately.

The Question of Borders

At a conference organised by his party, Rafi,[3] in Tel Aviv in August 1967 Dayan declared, 'The primary issue before us is that of Israel's boundaries'. This was a momentous remark. To the degree that Dayan could obligate Mapai, his former and future political home, he was setting out a new national agenda, at the centre of which lay the establishment of new borders for Israel. Since the end of the War of Independence the question of borders had not concerned the Israeli public, not even the Herut party, except for a passing moment after the Sinai campaign. People regarded the borders as they then were as permanent, and applied themselves to improving their economic position as individuals and to the advancement of the state within the existing frontiers. Now a far-reaching change, brought out by pressure from below, occurred in the very centre of Israeli politics. In a formal sense, the change was expressed in the aforementioned proposals regarding peace terms, which were adopted without opposition. In practice it took the form of a slow but systematic expansion of Jewish settlements in the occupied territories. Yigael Allon, one of the prominent ministers in Eshkol's government, even went so far as to present a plan accompanied by a detailed map, according to which the West Bank was to be divided between Israel and Jordan, thus indicating that Dayan was not the only one to hold this view. When the question of borders was placed at the top of Israel's priorities, the only prominent statesman who sensed where a national agenda centred around borders would lead — as he had perceived the significance of events in the past — was David Ben-Gurion. In return for peace, he proposed withdrawal to the 4 June 1967 borders, with the exception of Jerusalem. Apart from correcting the 'eternally lamentable failure', — his phrase for the failure to break through the walls of the Old City of Jerusalem in 1948 — Ben-Gurion wanted nothing. He knew that the government's proposals were bound to lead to a bi-national state in which Jewish independence would be lost and the basic values which he had advocated since his arrival in Palestine, such as Jewish labour including hard physical labour, would be eroded.

Between June 1967 and the end of 1968 the elements of a new national agenda took shape: the aspiration to establish permanent expanded borders to include portions of Palestine occupied by Arabs within the map of the country, although not in a way formalised by international law; and further, the emphasis upon military power as the mainstay of national existence. The importance of the latter had never been in doubt, but against the background of the war, and in view of Israel's comparative position before and after it, the IDF rose several degrees in the hierarchy of national values. Moreover, the victory solved the problems of the economy: within less than two years after the outbreak of the war — it will be recalled that it broke out in the depths of a severe recession — the country responded with furious economic activity. Real income rose. There was full employment, and it even became necessary to draw on manpower from the conquered territories to supply the economy's growing need for workers. Along with these developments certain patterns of co-existence with the Arabs from the territories emerged, at the centre of which stood a firm but relaxed, even benevolent, military government. Within two years the characteristic traits of Dayan's policies were visible in Judea, Samaria, and the Gaza Strip, including the free flow of goods and people across the Jordan River bridges, free movement within the whole area under Israeli control, and employment for anyone who wanted to work. (This channelled some of the resources then flowing into Israel towards the Arab population; it is difficult to imagine a better method of quashing the desire to revolt than by drowning it in a torrent of money.) Dayan was not alone in calculating that this would be the permanent pattern for the internal settlement between Jews and the Arab inhabitants of Palestine, a pattern which could last for ever.

The Dayan Era

How did it come about at this juncture in the nation's history that the government was identified not with the man at its head but with the Minister of Defence, who represented, if one may say that Dayan represented any institution, a minority party which was in the process of eliminating itself? Moreover, why should the first formulation of the new national agenda be attributed to him, as well as the creation of a pattern of life for Jews and Arabs in a state which was in fact jointly theirs? The answer is that at that time and until the Yom Kippur War, Dayan was what we now call the 'King of Israel' in the eyes of the Israeli public, of diaspora Jewry, and of the non-Jewish world. In his years of glory, he spoke for the liberal left — by virtue of his advocacy of a humane and enlightened attitude towards the Arabs — and for the nationalist right, who correctly understood that he was in fact implementing their dream of the entire Land of Israel. He was borne aloft on the waves of affection and respect which had been Ben-Gurion's during the first decade of the state's existence. At that time he seemed omnipotent, and his miraculous rescue from a landslide that had buried him merely strengthened the impression that the hand of Providence was stretched out over him. Obviously some people gnashed their teeth in anger at seeing Dayan raised to such heights, but that gnashing of teeth was ineffectual: the man seemed to be beyond the reach of his political rivals.

Anyone who kept close track of Dayan's words and actions during his heyday, before he was caught out making obscure statements indicating an inability to cope with the predictable contradictions in which his policies became entangled, could already distinguish the basic features of his thinking. The first was sitting on the fence. When exposed, he would cover himself by ambiguous statements, which were the opposite of what one expected from a straight-talking Sabra (native-born Jewish Israeli).

Here is an example from the speech to his party conference quoted above: 'The territories we have taken, including the Suez Canal and the Golan Heights, are precious to us. But they differ from the cradle of our history, Hebron, Shilo, and Anatot'. After that introduction one would expect a conclusion in keeping with the government's decision that the mandatory borders should become the boundaries of the State of Israel, and that Dayan was recommeding the annexation of the West Bank, no matter what formula he chose. However, he added, 'It is not a question of borders and Lebensraum. It is much deeper and more binding than our connection with the other territory we have conquered'. Then, after mentioning the bond between the Bible and the Land of the Bible, what was his practical conclusion? 'The right to pray at the Tomb of the Patriarchs in Hebron, the right to live together [with the Arabs] in the cradle of our culture'. He concluded with a sentence that left the listener in limbo: 'These are not political programmes but something much stronger than political programmes — they are the dreams of a nation which have come true'. But the same pressing questions remained: what was to be done with the West Bank from a political point of view? Must it be placed under Israeli sovereignty, or was it merely necessary to permit Jews to pray at the Tomb of the Patriarchs? Must they simply have the right to live in the cradle of their culture, regardless of whether as its owners or as guests, even permanent guests? In an experience like a dream, there is in fact no need to provide a clear-cut answer, but Dayan was a statesman, and an outstanding one, when he made that speech. He posed obscure questions to which he supplied obscure and ambiguous answers with as many meanings as there were interpreters.

As we have said, Dayan placed the issue of the borders at the top of the national agenda. But in a lecture which he gave in the summer of 1969 he showed his true self in a powerful personal confession.[4] Those who knew him knew that Moshe Dayan was speaking here as he really was, without the ceremonial mask of the general and the politician. In that lecture, entitled 'Fear Not, My Servant Jacob', an existentialist's creed was revealed, negating the very question of purpose. Purpose, even in the life and prosperity of a nation, is not worthy of our attention, although it is natural to seek it. The only subject which need concern us, the one which uniquely concerned the lecturer, was the existential struggle 'for which we have been destined throughout all generations'. Thence the unique and single imperative: Let us continue to struggle. So that its spirit would not flag nor its hands weaken, the following words, both mild and severe at the same time, were spoken to the nation: 'Fear not, my servant Jacob'. Within the arid and chill expanse of that lecture, there was no place for borders. There were no historic rights, not to mention security in any concrete sense — not exactly what one would expect of someone who was not just any politician, but a popular leader. The lecture presented an abstract struggle for existence, without any visible cause or defined purpose, in effect, struggle for its own sake. That personal and austere message, though it was full of glory and courage, could not, in the final analysis, fulfil the public's need for political answers. Dayan's alteration of the structure and values of Israeli policy was therefore made specific later on by Menachem Begin and the disciples of the late Rabbi Ysvi Yehuda Kook (the theological authority most influential among the religious settlers in the West Bank), who knew and stated clearly what was black and what was white.

The War of Attrition

Although during its early years Israel's sovereignty was of a very special sort in that the state lacked fixed borders, its first wars, both in 1948 and 1956, were normal wars: they began on a certain date and ended on another. The armies that participated in them ceased firing at each other. True, after 1951 there were a large number of infiltrators from the south, the east, and the north who stole, killed, and committed acts of sabotage and espionage. However, these acts were committed by irregular forces which, while they enjoyed the support of countries which claimed they were still in a state of war with Israel, did not aim at military victory or conquest. The infiltrators came and went, making every effort not to encounter the Israeli security forces. There were exceptions. In the early 1950s skirmishes took place between the IDF and the Jordanian army, and in 1964 there were exchanges of fire with the Syrian army, but these were isolated incidents which had little effect on daily life. In this sense they were like the infiltration mentioned above: for the vast majority of the Israeli public they were basically reading matter in the newspapers.

This was no longer the case after the Six Day War. After a short period of respite, a continuous series of hostilities took place on a considerable scale. Along the Suez Canal the Egyptians opened fire which only subsided to begin again the next day. In mid-1968 hardly a week passed, and, for a while, hardly a day, when the Israeli newspapers did not publish the photographs of young men — their faces clearly showed they were conscripts — killed by Egyptian fire. Between 1968 and 1970 the Israeli public became acquainted with a new kind of war, a war of attrition, in which armies never stop firing on each other. Israel did not turn the other cheek. The IDF attacked Egypt on land, including daring amphibious raids, and from the air. In 1969–70 the bombing became so intense that the Egyptians were forced to call for Soviet assistance to defend the skies over their capital and the airspace over the Canal.

The War of Attrition came to an end in August 1970 through the intervention of the great powers, who feared the outbreak of a full-scale war. However, the years between 1968 and 1970 left the ineradicable impression of war as a constant presence which made its mark on public life by the grievous loss of life and the economic effort needed to maintain an armistice line which was not quiet for a moment.

The Internal Debate

Consequently, the war became a subject of public debate of the first order, about which opinions differed widely. Some recalled the exaltation of June 1967, the lightning victory and the expansion of political horizons in its aftermath. They saw the achievements of the war as prized possessions, and their retention worthy of any sacrifice over any length of time. Others argued that, since even the crushing victory of the Six Day War had not brought peace any nearer, a compromise must be sought, including the return of conquered territory, in order to put an end to the slaughter, the suffering, and the material destruction. Henceforth the division between doves and hawks came to dominate Israeli politics, as opposed to the traditional division between capitalists and proletarians or secular and religious Jews. The reason was clear: in that war was becoming a central national experience, attitudes towards it naturally became the primary identifying marks of the citizen's or politician's place in the political spectrum.

Inevitably the question which had concerned many people *before* the establishment of the state constantly recurred: is co-existence between Jews and Arabs possible? The answer to that question was sought particularly energetically by those who held that the conquests of the Six Day War were not bargaining counters, i.e. not possessions in return for which Israel would gain other advantages if and when the Arab countries rescinded the resolutions of the Khartoum Conference and entered into peace negotiations. Moshe Dayan and growing numbers of Israelis therefore concentrated their attention on the issue of co-existence. From their point of view the Land of Israel — and later the Golan Heights and portions of the Sinai Peninsula — were not for sale. Since those regions of the Land of Israel, — Judea and Samaria and the Gaza Strip — were densely populated by Arabs, the issue of the legal status of that population as individuals and as a group imposed itself upon public opinion, on the political community, and on the government. Thus another component was added to the national agenda, although those who advocated the return of all or most of the territories would certainly have wished to prevent its inclusion. Perhaps the effort to prevent the erasure of the Green Line (the pre-5 June armistice line) would have received wider public support if it had not become increasingly clear that, even in the very best possible case, one was speaking in terms of an extremely prolonged temporary state — for years went by and not a single Arab state was found willing to fly in the face of the three 'Noes' of Khartoum.

Logically it was the doves who had to revise one of the basic assumptions common in Israel before the Six Day War, namely the view that Arab hostility was a fact of nature. The desire to compromise, which arose, among other things, from the doves' recognition of the difficulties of co-existence with an Arab population of 1.2–1.3 million, demanded that partners in dialogue be found. But the very idea of dialogue had to be based on the assumption that not only was there someone to whom one could speak or that such a partner could be found in the foreseeable future, but that this interlocutor would also be guided by reason and be prepared to be influenced by political arguments. That is, the doves were forced by their own logic to abandon the view that Arab hostility was a given which could not be altered by Israeli policy, with or without the good offices of intermediaries.

The political debate within Israel led to two complementary results and overturned certain opinions which had enjoyed general acceptance prior to the Six Day War. The hawks accepted the Palestinian Arabs as citizens of the country, though not exactly in the legal sense, including the Druze of the Golan Heights and the Beduin of the Sinai Peninsula; in contrast, the doves included the Arab states in the political community with which contact and dialogue must be initiated in order to resolve political disputes. This process led to a convergence of opinions that were seemingly polar opposites and contributed to the de-demonisation of the Arabs. From an inexplicable and uncontrollable phenomenon of nature, they became the potential object of widely diverse political approaches ranging from war, through the establishment of majority-minority relations, to making peace.

One cannot exaggerate the depth and extent of the change which took place in Israel in the aftermath of the Six Day War. The national agenda, which was dynamic up to 1960 but increasingly frozen until the war, had a single issue at its core, the construction and strengthening of the Jewish community from within. The wars which took place in that period did not alter that emphasis. Perhaps this would have remained the case after 1967, had Israel been guided by a vigorous national agenda. But the war fell upon the nation and its leaders while they were suspended in limbo. Thus the new agenda shaped by the war and its aftermath was established with little difficulty.

As we have said, the war, its achievements and the challenges it presented became the principal items in the new national agenda. Another component, a creation of the times, was also included: the sense of power projected beyond the borders of the state. In the early 1950s Ben-Gurion had considered asking for Israel's inclusion in NATO, a notion based less on what Israel might contribute to the alliance beyond making its territory available to the hoped-for partnership, than on the additional security which the alliance would provide. From 1967 on this was no longer the case. A glance at the map was sufficient to show that Israel had become a regional power extending from the Suez Canal to Sharm Al-Sheikh in the south, sitting only a few dozen kilometers from Damascus, and controlling the Saudi oil pipeline (the Tapline, debouching in Tripoli in Lebanon) in the north. Israel had just vanquished in less than a week, a coalition of the three strongest Arab armies and, moreover, its air force possessed strategic capabilities. To illustrate the feeling that Israel had become a power, one should recall that Yigael Allon, who, in terms of the period, tended to the doveish side, seriously considered establishing a Druze state under Israel's protection. At the time Israel provided the main support for the Kurdish rebellion in Iraq. In 1970 it acted in co-ordination with the United States to deter Syria from intervening in the war waged by King Hussein of Jordan against the Palestine Liberation Organisation, which sought to seize power east of the Jordan. The changes wrought by the war, following which the Arabs in the areas under direct Israeli control as well as those in the Arab states became an object of policy, Israel's strong position in the region, and the accompanying feeling of being a power — all this transformed Israel beyond all recognition and persuaded the public to adopt an agenda which had not existed during the 1950s, even in embryo.

In early 1965 the Herut Movement and the Liberal Party established a political bloc, in reaction to the establishment of the 'New Alignment' of Mapai and Ahdut Haavoda. Yosef Sapir and his comrades within the General Zionist Party viewed the step taken by Levi Eshkol and Yisrael Galili as finally blocking the way for any centre-left coalition. The response came in two stages: the General Zionists dissolved their partnership with the Progressive Party, with whom they had gone to the polls in the elections to the fifth Knesset in 1961 as the Liberal Party; they then established a new electoral bloc in partnership with Herut — Gahal (a Hebrew acronym).

Those who would believe that strict laws govern the events of history may reflect on what might have happened if the President of Egypt had not committed the error — some say act of madness — of mounting a challenge to Israel's existence in May 1967. At the time the problems of the economic recession preoccupied the Israeli public to the exclusion of all other concerns. There were no signs that the end of the crisis was in sight and, in any event, to put an end to it would have taken considerable time and entailed many difficulties. This hypothetical process would certainly have made the crisis within Mapai more acute, and the leading party in the coalition would have had to face the voters in 1969 in a weakened condition, saddled, as it were, with the burden of economic recession and unemployment unprecedented since the establishment of the state. Opposing it would have been the Herut-Liberal bloc with a very different economic approach, offering its own national agenda with a strong nationalist tinge — although not an operational one, if one can judge from the silencing of Herut's claim to the East bank of the Jordan and even to the West Bank — but primarily bearing a clear economic and social message. There is reason to believe that if that had been the course of events, with an electoral contest against the background of the economic crisis, the new bloc would have taken most of its character from the General Zionist element. And it is not wildly fantastic to envisage Yosef Sapir, who was then in his prime, as a major leader and ultimately the head of Gahal as it led an alternative coalition government.

However, that was not the course taken by events. President Nasser prolonged Mapai's life, although Mapai (later the Labour Party) did little to justify his generosity apart from re-admitting Moshe Dayan into its ranks and partially and hesitantly reconciling itself to the new national agenda mainly created by him. This brought about a change in the balance of power within Gahal: its nationalism sprang to renewed life as the memory of the recession faded. Its historical platform, laying claim to the entire Land of Israel, was now about to materialise thanks to the IDF's conquests, and to gain ascendance until ultimately Herut received its final legitimisation from the man best suited to grant it — Moshe Dayan, who declared that Menachem Begin was closer to him than Meir Yaari (the leading ideologist of the leftist Hashomer Hatsair movement and by then a member of the Labour Alignment). Dayan's remarks had been made in a limited political context, but in two senses they were the honest truth considering the man who made them: Mapam and the historical leftism of the *kibbutz* party had never meant much to Dayan, the statist *moshavnik*; and although he abhorred Begin's nationalist pathos, the two saw eye to eye on the inclusion of all of the Land of Israel under Israeli sovereignty. The tactical differences between the two as to the ways and means of achieving this could not obscure the identity between them on the main point of the new national agenda.

As noted, in practical terms Nasser granted a reprieve to Mapai-Labour rule, which Mapai used to bolster its much weakened position by adapting itself to the new attitudes now gaining currency in the public mind and the new national agenda. Changes in leadership also promoted the process of adaptation: Levi Eshkol died in early 1969, and his place as Prime Minister was taken by Golda Meir. Unlike her predecessor, she was not easily tempted to believe that any change had taken place in Arab public opinion or in the attitudes of the Arab leadership, which would open the way for a political settlement with the Arab countries. She re-established the national unity government of June 1967, thus reaffirming, of her own free will, the programme that had been agreed upon under duress in conditions of national emergency. She also ratified the aforementioned process of adaptation which one cannot imagine would have taken place if the left, led by the Labour Party, had had a valid national agenda of its own. But, since such an agenda was lacking, and Gahal saw no reason to abandon a satisfactory partnership, it stayed in the government, and so, with no real opposition to the national agenda then in force, the 1969 elections proceeded in a low-key manner.

A few examples from this period illustrate the atmosphere of ennui and the absence of political contest between the major parties. About a month and a half before the elections, on 28 September 1969, Eliezer Livne, who in his latter years had become one of the most prominent intellectual proponents of the movement for the Land of Israel, wrote in *Haaretz*: 'The elections for the seventh Knesset inaugurate no new stage: they are the final step in the degeneration of an old situation'. He added, 'It is sufficient to say that the Labour Party has betrayed its essential goals . . . of proposing a national policy and selecting leaders'. Two weeks later, on 17 October, Yoel Marcus wrote in the same newspaper: 'For the first time the election campaign lacks any challenge or central issue'. And Yeremiyahu Yovel, one of the rising publicists among the doves, entitled his article on that very subject in *Haaretz* of 21 October 'Elections without Controversy'. These quotations might appear somewhat exaggerated. For professional reasons journalists like sharp definitions and ideological disputes, both of which are hateful to politicians. But a retrospective analysis confirms the then prevailing view: the election campaign of 1969 was shadow-boxing. It could not be anything else, for it was conducted on the basis proposed by Dayan, which Gahal found no difficulty in supporting, and with which the Labour Party agreed for lack of any alternative of its own. Dayan expressed the substance of the new national agenda in an election speech on 27 October: 'Our main purpose is to make the new territories into Israeli territories'.

Had the elections been held at the end of 1970 and not a year earlier, they would not have lacked a central issue; and this only goes to show how greatly political controversies and decisions are influenced by external events which are not necessarily predictable. In August 1970 a cease-fire along the Suez Canal came into effect (and afterwards along the cease-fire line with Syria also). Under the terms of the cease-fire, Israel agreed to declare its acceptance of Security Council Resolution 242, according to which it had to withdraw from conquered territories. Since 1967 that resolution had been a subject of endless controversy because the English and French texts can be construed differently; the English version can be interpreted to mean that Israel has to withdraw from some, but not all, of the conquered territories, whereas the French version seems to order Israel to withdraw from all of them. In Menachem Begin's view the entire Resolution was bad — he changed this view only upon being named Prime Minister in 1977; he therefore led Gahal out of the coalition. It stands to reason that Begin would have made the Resolution and its ratification by the government into a central campaign issue in an election contested by candidates divided between those prepared to withdraw in return for peace and recognition and those insisting on the annexation of the West Bank as a minimum, whatever the price.

A second issue, poverty and ethnicity, also arrived on the scene too late for the 1969 elections. We have already mentioned that before the 1959 elections the subject arose and then faded away. Ten years later it did not even arise. But since May 1971 it has not left the political agenda. Nevertheless, the problem of poverty and ethnicity never became a central or decisive issue, nor did it determine the identity or character of the government, mainly because all the parties declared themselves willing to solve it and, in effect, to make it disappear.

Given the broad agreement about the existence of the problem and the need to solve it, it might seem surprising that such a long time was needed before it received conscious attention: more than twenty years passed in the life of a sovereign society in which the voter was able to influence the government directly, before the issue was identified and publicly discussed. A probable reason for the tardiness in identifying the issue is that the political community lacked intellectual categories for grasping both aspects of the subject. During Israel's first two decades both the right and the left arrayed themselves on either side of the line separating employers and self-employed, on the one hand, and wage-earners, on the other. This Marxian scheme, both in its radical and its social-democratic versions, divided the world between those who live only by their own labours and everyone else, and the distinction was accepted by the right as well, although without accepting the conclusions drawn by the left. Poverty has only been discovered in post-Marxian society, that is, the consumer society, in which the poor are defined as those who do not receive their due share of the general abundance of goods and services.

Since Mapai had shed its socialist beliefs years before, it had little difficulty in making the ideological transition from the worker-capitalist to the poor-rich dichotomy. Yitzhak Ben-Aharon, for example, as the Secretary of the Histadrut, an organisation whose entire existence was justified by the division between workers and employers, gave a great deal of attention to poverty and its problems. The other parties followed Mapai's lead. However, they all needed a push to start thinking in terms of poverty and affluence, and, even before that, the objective conditions for such a way of thinking needed to come into existence. Until the late 1960s it is doubtful whether one could regard Israel as a relatively affluent society. And this is the necessary background for the distinction between the affluent and those who live in an affluent society without sharing its benefits — in other words, their housing is substandard and their incomes are low and irregular.

As for the ethnic component, its very mention must be seen as a violation of the Zionist creed accepted throughout the political community and according to which there is not and cannot be any distinction between one Jew and another, not to mention discrimination brought about deliberately or by neglect. However by 1971 the problem, or rather consciousness of the problem, surfaced and imposed itself on public opinion. It seems quite likely that originally the issue was imported from the United States, where from the mid-1960s onward a growing campaign had been waged for equal civil rights for blacks who in a short time also came to be known as the poor. In other words, in the United States, two social movements were fused. The first fought for civil rights, the second for the improvement of the economic lot of the blacks and Martin Luther King, the black Protestant minister who headed the movement, sought to combine the struggle against racial discrimination with the struggle to improve the economic situation of the black population. Information about the black struggle for civil rights reached Israel with the thousands of students who returned to the country after completing their studies in the United States, and it made an increasingly strong impression there. In the late 1960s the process of Americanisation was in full swing in Israel: anyone seeking legitimisation for a cultural or political innovation felt obliged to find it in an American model. This was the background for the apparently surprising fact that a group of young people of Moroccan descent in the Musrara neighbourhood of Jerusalem called themselves 'Panthers', after the Black Panthers in the United States.

In early January 1971 the leftwing newspaper *Al Hamishmar* published an article about the group under the headline 'We will be Israel's Black Panthers'. The article said that the Panthers would fight the government, the Ashkenazis, and the establishment. One of the activists was quoted, apparently in connection with the trial of the Jews in Leningrad accused of hijacking an airliner: 'When they hanged black Jews in Baghdad, the Ashkenazis kept quiet. Now, when they are planning to hang white Jews in Russia, they go on hunger strikes and everybody is out demonstrating'. In itself this statement constituted a heretical denial of the main tenet of Zionism — Jewish solidarity under all conditions. Further talks with the activists showed that, in addition to accusing the government and the establishment of ethnic discrimination, they exhibited great bitterness over economic discrimination, particularly in housing. The copy of the American model was thus complete: claims of racial discrimination — ethnic discrimination in the Israeli version — combined with economic discrimination. No wonder the Panthers' demonstrations were quickly joined by activists from Siah and Matzpen, two ultra leftish groups which, in addition to being 100 per cent Ashkenazi, combined anti-Zionism with a sensitive social conscience. Thus the New Left, the radicals, in Israel as in the United States, discovered that the combination of poverty and ethnicity could be used as a stick with which to beat the affluent society.

The New Left was not alone in being interested in the subject. In 1971, a vintage year for social awareness in Israel, the affluent society, though only relatively so, took up the question of poverty, defined as a deficiency in consumption, and its identifying mark, ethnic discrimination. One of many examples indicating this concern was a series of articles by Eliahu Salpeter in *Haaretz*, perhaps the first exhaustive treatment of the subject of social divisions to appear in the Israeli press. In these articles Salpeter concentrated on the visible symptoms of the problem: the relative disadvantages of the Oriental Jews in education and housing, which he presented as comprehensive manifestations of the income diffe-rential between Jews of European and American origin and those born in Israel as against immigrants from Asia and Africa. It is noteworthy that he did not mention the feelings of deracination and disorientation which came in the aftermath of the transition from a traditional community to a modern society, or the condescending attitudes of the veteran residents to the new immigrants, both of which combined to arouse and foster hatred against the Ashkenazis. This was a strange omission, for if there was hatred it should have been foremost among the problems demanding discussion. In any event, the Israeli establishment had long since and willingly accorded a high priority to closing the gaps in housing (and in income generally) and in education. But there was no conscious treatment of the psychological effects, namely the anger and hatred arising out of differences in levels of consumption or the coldness of the veterans towards the new arrivals. Perhaps this was because in a materialist society problems can only be defined quantitatively. However that may be, from 1971 onwards the issue of poverty and ethnicity was included in the national agenda — not as a primary issue like that of the borders, but as a secondary one, whose importance in internal politics could no longer be ignored.

In the wake of the victory in the Six Day War and the effective expansion of Israel's borders, a new national agenda came into being, based on political values which had not been accepted until then except by marginal public figures. Nor was the voice of those loyal to 'Little Israel', within the borders of 4 June 1967, heard; they were pushed aside by circumstances and placed on the defensive. The resolutions of the Khartoum conference and the massive rearmament undertaken by the Arab states shortly after the battle died down blocked the way to negotiations. At the same time, the ease with which the barriers between the Arab inhabitants of the West Bank and the Israeli occupation forces fell, as well as the flood of workers from the newly occupied territories seeking employment in Israel, blinded many people, including those apprehensive about territorial over-expansion, given that the population of these territories were not granted equal political and economic status.

Nevertheless, the achievements of the war, which vindicated the hawks and swelled their ranks, did not completely empty the camp of the doves. For historical reasons they were concentrated in the Labour Party, sharing the sense that Israel was getting too big for its own good, disturbed by the appearance of Arabs from the territories in a society that had been overwhelmingly Jewish until the war, and fearing that Israel had entered an arena where only great powers can contend without coming to grief. In addition to the initial unhappiness and apprehension, there were practical reasons later on for opposition, at first passive and then active, to the policy of expanded borders and its perceived consequence — continued war. The principal reasons were the rising material cost of maintaining an effective state of war and, even more, the casualties, those killed and maimed in the exchanges of fire along the Suez Canal, the pursuits in the Jordan Valley, and the skirmishes in the north.

Why did the doves congregate in the Labour Party? It should be borne in mind that that party was identified with the State of Israel of 1949, that since the 1930s its members had never been deluded by notions of a bi-national state (either socialist or imperial) and that a good number of its leaders, as typified by the Finance Minister, Pinhas Sapir, were responsible for the proper functioning of the economy and thus fearful about the economic cost of a Greater Israel. Moreover, many Labour members opposed the policy because they despised its prime mover, Moshe Dayan. He belonged to their party, had been born and brought up in it, but he was considered, and perhaps rightly, to be one who had left it for greener pastures.

These establishment doves were in a double bind. They were members of a party which, willingly or otherwise, bore the burden of government and did not wish to give up its perquisites. What is more, the Arabs took no visible notice of them. On the contrary, from 1968 onwards, the Arab states, led by Egypt, having rapidly recovered from the shock of their military defeat, initiated positonal warfare on the Egyptian front along the Suez Canal and a guerrilla war along the Jordan and inside Israel. Both forms of war were intended to compel Israel to withdraw, rather than to achieve withdrawal through negotiations. As noted earlier, the logic of the doves' position had to be based on the assumption that there was a possibility of coming to terms with the neighbouring states; but until President Nasser's death in the autumn of 1970, there was nothing to support that assumption. In 1971 President Sadat did put out feelers aimed at breaking the deadlock: he proposed a partial settlement, with Israeli withdrawal to the interior of the Sinai Peninsula in return for a kind of cease-fire. But in the meantime two of the practical arguments used by the doves to justify their desire for an agreement had disappeared. From August 1970 the fighting along the Suez Canal had died down, and with it, the loss of life. And the PLO which had been responsible for the guerrilla warfare along the Jordan and within Israel, had been defeated in fierce battles with the Jordanian army and was engaged in the process of reorganisation in Lebanon. At the same time, US aid began to flow into Israel, in effect reducing the cost of security to the Israeli taxpayer.

Consequently, the establishment doves had no practical arguments against holding on to a Greater Israel extending from the Golan Heights in the north to the Red Sea in the south, from the Jordan in the east to the Mediterranean in the west; this seemed to be feasible at a little cost in life or money. Although they could point out the risks, both political and moral, entailed in the creation of a bi-national state, their arguments carried little weight against the advantages inherent in the *status quo*: the security zone provided by the conquered territories and the increased supply of manpower needed by a growing economy. Many members of the doveish opposition therefore quit the political arena, where disputes are settled by votes on the basis of more or less rational arguments, and moved into another arena, in a sense a pre-political one: that of protest, where individuals form *ad hoc* groups, and where the criterion for success is the ability to attract attention.

Thus, for example, seventy high school graduates from Jerusalem sent a letter to the Prime Minister in the spring of 1970, before their call-up in the IDF. They wrote, 'We do not know whether we shall be able to do as we are ordered in the army, under the slogan, "There is no choice"'. The occasion for this letter was Prime Minister Golda Meir's refusal to permit Nahum Goldman, the President of the World Jewish Congress, to visit Cairo and sound out President Nasser as to the possibility of negotiations with Egypt. It should be added, to emphasise the astonishment provoked by the letter, that the signatories were sons of the social elite, which had taught them unconditional patriotism, and they included the son of a future minister, the son of an eminent professor at the Hebrew University, and so on. Traditionally young men of that kind had served in elite infantry and naval units and as fighter pilots. Now they voiced doubts concerning the rightness and morality of the Israeli cause and their own willingness to follow orders unquestioningly.

While some of those about to be called up and sent to the front were expressing their protest in advance, those who had already been there sang 'The Song of Peace' at the tops of their voices. This song had been written by a soldier who lost a leg, someone who indeed knew what he was talking about — and the death of young men in the prime of their lives, death stripped of the romance of battle, has always drawn a response from the civilised world. Hence the powerful resonance it struck among the social elites. A journalist later recalled an evening in an army camp where a convention of Nahal (army units spending part of their service as farmers on collective settlements) was held, and where those present, from the commanding officer of Nahal to the least of privates, not to speak of the guests, all sang 'The Song of Peace' with enthusiasm. Further protest against the never ending war was also expressed in a play called, 'The Queen of the Bathtub'. Unlike 'The Song of Peace', the play, whose author called it a satirical review, was not greeted with tolerance, almost certainly because of its coarse language, taken from the graffiti on the walls of public lavatories. But the content of the play was authentic, and perhaps the coarseness as well, an expression of the brutality of war. At any rate, Israeli society was not pleased with its own face in that mirror, whether it was accurate or distorted. The playwright, Hanoch Levine, did not dwell only on the war: most of the scenes dealt with subjects like man's inhumanity to man, ethnic discrimination, the exploitation of the Arabs, or simply spiritual emptiness. But what struck an especially raw nerve was a take-off of the Bible story in which Abraham prepares to cut the throat of his son Isaac for obscure reasons, closing his ears to the voice of God, who offers him a ram in place of his son. The message got across but the playwright also explained, for the benefit of the obtuse, that he was referring to fathers who sent their sons to die in battle, unwilling to hear about other ways of settling the dispute with their neighbours.

The protest activities had several common traits, including the rejection of values which had hitherto been immune from public questioning, such as Israel's rightness in the dispute with its neighbours, the main issue of which was, according to the common view, the Jewish state's right to exist, and the readiness to die in battle symbolised the Israeli's moral superiority to his neighbours (rather ingeniously, it was held that the fallen died so that the nation might live). Moreover, doubts arose as to the morality of co-existence between people living in material plenty, the soldiers existing in the shadow of death along the cease-fire lines, and the exploited Arabs in the occupied territories. Like the awakening to the issue of ethnicity and poverty, which also began in the early 1970s, anti-war protest too was a fashionable import. The United States, the source of all political and cultural imports since the 1960s, was in the throes of a political crisis in the early 1970s — perhaps the deepest of its post-civil war history — as a result of a war which it could not win but was loath to lose. Demonstrations by veterans, the burning of draft cards, and the return of medals were the identifying marks of a political crisis which produced a counter-culture of protest which expressed itself in every walk of life. The American example provided models of protest and triggered similar processes in Israel. One cannot understand the protest movements in Israel after the Yom Kippur War without seeing them as a continuation of what had begun to grow up at a time when consciousness of military superiority was still a treasured possession of the Israel public.

US Aid

The United States provided vital aid to Israel at its inception: diplomatic recognition and a loan of $100 million during its first year, without which the new state would have had a hard time getting through the early stages of self-construction. The aid was given primarily thanks to the lobbying of the large and influential Jewish community, but also in no small measure because of the general sympathy enjoyed by Israel in the country at large — as opposed to the business leaders and the political community — due to its democratic character and its image as a brave, pioneering nation. However, the two countries kept their political distance: the American Jewish community assumed the task of providing economic assistance to their brethren in Israel, but the US super-power remained aloof. American business leaders and the military and political establishment, amply represented at the higher levels of the State Department and the Pentagon, had always been dubious about Israel, believing that unduly close relations with the country would interfere with their ties with the Arabs. This chilly attitude suited Israel's Prime Ministers during the 1950s. Apart from David Ben-Gurion's non-committal exploration of possible adherence to NATO, no one in Israel advocated close political ties with the United States.

However, Soviet penetration in the area, starting in the mid-1950s, caused a change on both sides. The US political establishment, or rather parts of it, began to show a strategic interest in Israel because of its geographical position. Israel too felt the need for a defence against the overwhelming power of the Soviet Union, which was demonstrating increasing hostility towards the Jewish state which it had helped to bring into being no less than the United States. The Six Day War and its outcome turned Israel into a regional power, but it also exacerbated Soviet hostility. Hence a mutual interest developed on the part of Israel and the United States, an interest which received tangible expression in President Johnson's promise to supply Israel, for the first time in the history of relations between the two countries, with first-line weapons systems, Phantom fighter planes.

However, the fundamental shift in relations between the two countries took place later, during the Nixon Administration. Involvement in the war in Vietnam and the social unrest that plagued the United States deepened in the 1960s, affecting its global status adversely. President Nixon, more than his predecessor, recognised the need for alliances to plug strategic gaps left by the US withdrawal from full global deployment. Israel, in its status as a regional power after the Six Day War, fitted Nixon's definition of a force that could assist in establishing and maintaining a barrier against the further expansion of Soviet influence in various parts of the world.

As for Israel, apart from its leaders' fears of the Soviet Union, it was confronting an insoluble problem as a result of the arms race that had begun immediately after the end of the battles of 1967: Israel lacked the necessary economic resources to maintain a military counterpoise, both quantitatively and qualitatively, to the Arab nations. American Jewry was unable to come to the rescue; from 1968 onward defence costs rocketed, reaching levels far above what had been known or expected in the past. An article by the present writer in *Haaretz* on 20 March 1970, defined the problem and proposed both a solution and the steps that should be taken to achieve it. The article is presented here in its entirety because it offers a fairly precise programme for deepening co-operation between the superpower and the country that later came to be seen as its representative in the Middle East, and the programme remains valid to this day.

Characteristically, relations between Israel and the United States are either in a state of euphoria or abysmal darkness. At the moment we are close to the low point, but will assuredly rise again — according to the strange laws governing these relations — and then we shall plunge into the depths again, and so on.

But more important than these swings is continuity over time and the sum total in substance of our bond with America. The United States has stood by us since our declaration of independence, assisted the establishment of our economy, and helped us to produce and purchase means for the defence of our state. It is doubtful whether there are many other countries which, without a treaty of any kind between them, have created such a firm bond between them as the United States and Israel.

This is the background to the ongoing debate regarding the fighter aircraft. One might hazard a guess based on twenty-three years of history, that until the Americans receive Soviet and Arab assent to the Rogers Plan, they will continue to assist us as they have done in the past. At the moment it is too soon to discuss how they might act if and when they receive that assent; Israel's political leadership should give some thought to the matter and plan countermeasures in advance. But in the meanwhile it is better for operational policies to be based on the assumption, commonly held by most Israeli politicians in any case, that the Russians and the Arabs do not favour Secretary of State Rogers' proposals. Thus in a while we shall once again be asking how much and what kind of assistance we can request from the United States, with a decent chance of our request being granted.

In last Wednesday's issue of *Haaretz* an article from the *New York Times* was quoted, reporting reasons given by US officials for their rejection of Israel's request for aircraft. Among other things the article says that, in their opinion, 'America cannot keep supplying weapons [to Israel] for ever'. This is idle chatter, however, for the quantities of weapons requested by Israel are small if a cost-benefit comparison is made between US supplies to Israel and to any other country. The question is not only about weapons but also about the creation of conditions which will allow Israel to stand firm as long as an environment conducive to negotiations rather than confrontation has not been created in the Middle East.

To be specific: we must emphasise our need for economic assistance at a rate of about $250 million a year for as long as our war with the Arabs continues. It is not only the pilot in his plane who fights but also the nation for which that pilot fights. There is no logical reason to harm the nation so long as it is agreed that the pilot must continue his task.

Although for the time being our request for the fighter aircraft was rejected, this should not weaken our resolve concerning the larger issue of assistance. From the political point of view this issue is no less sensitive. The Arabs too are circulating in the

West with their hands outstretched. As for explaining our needs in the United States, since in the final analysis the American taxpayer will be called upon to subsidise some of our expenses, it would seem that the matter is less difficult than it seems to many of the best among us. This does not imply that the money is there for the asking. It would be more correct to say that the presentation of reasonable requests combined with the raising of support among American public opinion and in the Congress (which is responsible for public expenditures) can produce the desired result.

Israel enjoys a degree of public credit among the Jews of America and among many non-Jews too. Like all credit, it is not unlimited. If one draws against it, by causing the absence of some congressmen from a speech by the President of France, for example, it is doubtful whether a sufficient amount will remain to motivate those same congressmen to vote in favour of economic aid to Israel. That is a schematic description of how political credit is drawn down and it suggests the conclusion that Israel must act according to a well thought out order of priorities if it wishes to obtain what it really needs from the United States.

Our first argument should be that a long war demands plentiful resources. Judging by the history of the Second World War, not a single country, except for the United States, was able to pay for the war on its own. Great Britain had to sell its assets and resort to American assistance; the Germans and the Japanese plundered the countries which they conquered, and even the Soviet Union requested and received aid from the West. This generalisation also applies to Israel. It paid for the Six Day War, speaking in general terms, by eliminating unemployment and by using up stocks. But the aftermath demanded resources which even the extremely generous contributions of the Jews in the diaspora cannot provide.

In the long term — and that is the term which our leaders advise us to consider — economic assistance is no less important than aircraft and tanks. However, an impression has been created, perhaps erroneously but nevertheless effectively, that we are only interested in weapons and not in resources in the broader sense of the term. One of the most important tasks of Israeli policy should be to make America attach greater importance and urgency to economic aid and to persuade the administration to honour our requests.

Obviously certain subjects under discussion between the United States and Israel should not be aired in public. In any case, silence does them no harm. However it is doubtful whether economic assistance belongs to that category, and it would seem that the subject ought to be given proper publicity. Here too one must act prudently. Just prior to the congressional elections (which will take place this November) may seem a poor time to make requests necessitating the allocation of public funds. But a tactical consideration of this sort should not prevent public discussion of the issue. Candidates, especially in areas where Israel is popular, should be made to take a position on it. That is not objectionable. In fact it is the only way to make the US administration act: public opinion must be influenced before the President and congressmen can relate to any issue, be it the construction of a highway between New York and Los Angeles or aid to Israel. The money we need does not grow on trees, nor is it allocated in consequence of private conversations between the Ambassador, Yitzhak Rabin, and officials in the State Department or the White House.

No one can claim, as could have been claimed a year ago, that Israel is seeking aid but living a life of luxury. Anyone with eyes to see and a bit of economic knowledge can understand that the policy known as a package deal imposes considerable hardships on the country and shows, that Israel is prepared to make sacrifices before it requests assistance. Israel must speak out about this and about its firm decision not to relinquish any territory before peace is assured. This is also the prevailing opinion in Washington. We must stress this consensus as long as it exists and ask the United States to aid us both politically and materially. From the experience of the twenty-three years since the establishment of the state one should learn that a logical argument on behalf of a policy which is in harmony with American interests, or which at least does not contradict them, can yield the desired results.

The State of Israel made a sustained effort to secure assistance in its protracted struggle with its neighbours and their Soviet patron. The United States responded, thus creating a model of co-operation between a superpower and its ally in the Middle East.

Notes

1. Moshe Dayan, *Milestones* (Hebrew) (Adanim-Nir, Yediot Aharonot Edition, Tel Aviv, 1976).

2. The 1955 Johnston Plan, negotiated by Ambassador Eric Johnston as President Eisenhower's special representative, superseded three projects drawn up in 1953. The Johnston Plan allocated approximately 60 per cent of the water of the Jordan River System to Lebanon, Syria and Jordan, and the remaining 40 per cent to Israel. Its technical aspects were approved by the Arab States and Israel, but in October 1955 it was rejected at a meeting of the Arab League.

3. Rafi, the Hebrew initials for the Israeli Workers List, was a breakaway group which seceded from Mapai in 1964, following Ben-Gurion's resignation. Among its more prominent members were Dayan and Peres. It participated in the 1965 Knesset elections, gaining about 8% of the vote entitling it to 10 members of the Knesset. It rejoined Mapai in 1968.

4. See *Haaretz*, 9 August 1969.

3 INTERMEZZO: INTO THE ABYSS

The Yom Kippur War does not belong directly to the story of the development of national agendas, the changes which took place in them and the change in government which came, sooner or later, in their wake. None the less the war was a historic landmark, well worth a brief glance, if only to observe the way two mainstays of the Jewish state functioned under stress. After the publication of the first part of the Report of the Commission under the chairmanship of Supreme Court Justice Shimon Agranat, appointed to inquire into the conduct of the war, many argued that its authors were excessively hard on the IDF. In that the report restricted itself to only three days of the war, and one front only, it could be claimed to have painted a distorted picture in which the errors committed by the IDF commanders on a single front were given too great prominence. It was further argued, and forcibly, that the IDF had been judged with excessive severity, and that the political leadership appeared to have been exonerated because the report had excluded the government and its functioning from the scope of their inquiry. However both these arguments miss the point. The Commission was not set up to celebrate a success, but rather to put its finger on the causes of a failure as perceived by the public; nor did it deserve to be reproached for concentrating on the period and theatre in which failure was most evident. As for the argument that the political leadership got off scot-free, it ignores the explicit assumption guiding the Commission, that the settling of accounts with the political leadership was a political matter. In fact the political system punished the country's leadership soundly; a month after the dismissal of the Chief of Staff, the Chief of Military Intelligence, the Commander of the Southern Front, etc., the Prime Minister, Golda Meir, and the Defence Minister, Moshe Dayan, were also obliged to resign, for having had the main responsibility for the government's handling of the war. The Minister of Defence, whom the public saw, not unjustifiably, as the man principally responsible not only for the management of the war but also for what had preceded it — including the failure to make decisions which might have prevented it — was more or less banished from

politics. Thus it is difficult to maintain that the investigation did not
further the cause of justice. In general terms rough and ready justice
was done; some might even go so far as to call it a lynching.

The Army's Failure

In retrospect, the army's failure was far greater and more thorough-
going than was suggested by the Agranat Report, especially as
regards the first rank of commanders in the IDF. The main source of
the failure was that the IDF had been prepared by its commanders
for the previous war, not for the one that was actually waged on the
southern and northern fronts in 1973. The failure had two roots: the
military capabilities of the Arab armies were misjudged, and the
optimal balance of forces and doctrine of warfare for the IDF were
not achieved. There is no need to analyse the Arab armies' military
abilities at length: they were well trained for the missions assigned
to them by the Egyptian and Syrian leaders. They did not break
even when the IDF recovered after the first onslaught and began to
force them back. In describing the war, Dayan repeatedly reports
these two features of the Arabs' performance. Another indication
of their improved capabilities emerges from the considerable losses
incurred by the IDF after it had broken through the Egyptian line at
the Canal, when the troops began to attack the Egyptian rear. At
that stage of the battle, typified by pursuit and raids on the enemy's
soft rear echelons, the IDF suffered serious loses: Dayan speaks of
eighty to ninety casualties a day. This was in dramatic contrast to the
experience of the Six Day War, which had provided the model for
the IDF command. In that war, once the enemy lines were penet-
rated, their armies simply fell apart.

The second error also belongs to what has been defined as
planning for the previous war. A structure of forces and combat
doctrine which had been valid in 1967 were applied to an army
which was obliged to fight under completely different conditions,
especially with regard to the battlefield function assigned to the air
force. The Six Day War was already virtually over in the early
morning hours on 5 June, when the Israeli air force destroyed those
of Egypt, Jordan, and Syria. Afterwards the Israeli ground troops
could advance freely on all fronts, whereas the Arab armies were
exposed to attack from the air. The assumption that the air force
could serve as airborne artillery in any war against the Arab armies

became an unquestioned axiom and a major component of the IDF combat doctrine.

In his book mentioned earlier, *Basic Surprise*, Tsvi Lanir describes war games conducted under the revealing code name of 'Iron Ram' by Southern Command in the summer of 1972, about a year before the war. These war games were predicated on an opening hypothesis which could rightly be called prophetic: four infantry divisions and nearly 400 enemy tanks were assumed to have crossed the Suez Canal with an advance warning of twenty-four hours; IDF reserve divisions did not enter the battle until the third day of the war. However, — and here is the difference between the war games and what actually happened — by the second day the regular army division stationed in Sinai was supposed to have fought the attackers to a standstill. 'On the third day', Lanir continues, *'while the air force controlled the skies over the Canal* (italics added), a reserve division under the command of General Adan crossed the Canal in the northern sector. On the fourth day, fighting had already begun on the west bank of the Canal'. The key lies in the words in italics: control of the air was a precondition for halting four divisions with one, and for the easy crossing of the Canal. However, since the air force did not control the skies over the Canal, either during the first days of the war or afterwards, the single regular army division was not strong enough to pin down the Egyptians once they had crossed to the east bank. Moreover, General Adan's counterattack on 9 October, which was supposed to take the IDF across to the west bank of the Canal, was doomed to failure.

Looking at the discrepancy between the war games and the war itself, the gravity of the mistaken estimate of the air force's capacity becomes devastatingly clear. Strangely, the ability of the air force to control the skies over the battle zone was never queried, although it was critical in order to stop the Egyptians and to cross the Canal early in the war. In 1969, at the end of the War of Attrition, the outcome of a conflict between fighter aircraft and a dense array of anti-aircraft missiles and cannon was already very much in doubt. The IDF staff officers of the Southern Command, who wrote the guidelines for their 'Iron Ram' war games, based them on fallacious reasoning. In other words, they set out with the desired result, a quick and elegant victory for the IDF, and they derived their basic data from it, especially the central pre-condition, the air force's absolute domination of the sky over the battlefield. This fallacy, shaped either by faulty logic or by intellectual dishonesty, could not fail to exact revenge on the IDF. The consequences of ignoring reality proved to be far graver than all the delays and negligence for which the Agranat Commission blamed the army command. In fact, there was only one front where the hopes placed in the air force as airborne artillery were justified: the north. When a Syrian armoured column came out from under its anti-aircraft umbrella in a hasty effort to penetrate the valley of the Sea of Galilee, it was caught by the air force and smashed.

In conclusion, then, the commanders of the IDF were not unjustly condemned and punished. Their loss of rank and prestige in the eyes of the public was deserved, although, as we have noted, not necessarily or primarily owing to the failures enumerated in the Agranat Commission Report. Later, people even questioned the accusation that the IDF had been taken by surprise, supposedly the main cause for its failure during the first few days of the war. Dayan himself wrote in *Milestones*, 'The advance warning was brief but did not come too late'. In the book referred to earlier, Lanir also demonstrates convincingly that in the Yom Kippur War there was no intelligence surprise, in other words it was not a situation typified by ignorance of the relevant facts, the knowledge of which was necessary for military action.

There is no simple answer to the question of how it happened that a body which, by its very *raison d'être*, ought to have been charac-terised by harsh realism (until the Yom Kippur War the IDF command was rigorously realistic in outlook) came to reconcile itself to a structure of forces and a military doctrine which had become outmoded. Certain of its officers had committed an error or become subject to a half-conscious self-delusion, as shown by the 'Iron Ram' war games. A basic flaw came to light which cannot be explained by the over-confidence of individuals: after all we are dealing here with a collective which is far from homogeneous intel-lectually or psychologically, and which is doctrinally obligated to act only after exhaustive and profound discussion prior to any decision. It can therefore be concluded that the entire organisation was affected by a collective process of deterioration in its critical facul-ties. This phenomenon is not unknown in cases where enormous success is followed by a sudden abundance in the resources available to an organisation — precisely what happened to the IDF between the two wars.

The Government's Failure

If that was true of the IDF, is it any wonder that the entire
government laboured under a delusion regarding the character of
the war which broke out on Yom Kippur? In principle, the Chief of
Staff is the government's military adviser, and the opinions which
were formed within the government following formal briefings were
consistent with what the Cabinet heard in their frequent informal
contacts with the military leadership. However, the Minister of
Defence, who wielded decisive authority within the government on
war matters, and who was also a military authority in his own right,
and, moreover, a sceptical and inquisitive person by nature, ought
to have noticed the dubious reality underlying the reassuring
answers given by the military leaders to questions asked by the
political leadership concerning the nature of the war which was
liable to break out in 1973. And he failed in this — certainly in *Milestones* there is no evidence of doubt, if indeed he harboured any prior
to the war, either with regard to the standard appraisal of the Arab
armies' military capacity or to the IDF's force structure and current
doctrine of warfare. Dayan was not alone in this failure, although
his acceptance of what was brought by the Chief of Staff to his
attention or for approval was decisive. Thus, for example, Yitzhak
Rabin[1] who was Chief of Staff during the Six Day War, in his
memoirs, *Service Record.* does not challenge either the IDF's
routine patterns of thought or their obsessive attachment to the Six
Day War as the only possible model of a major war with the Arab
nations. This is particularly surprising since in his memoirs Rabin
repeatedly emphasises the poor results of the air war over the Suez
Canal before the cease-fire agreement of August 1970. Thus both
Dayan and Rabin reveal the same blind spot: they did not see what
was right in front of their eyes. And if that was true of men like
Dayan and Rabin, it is not surprising that the entire government
failed to come to grips with military reality until the war made it
terrifyingly clear.

At the conference held in the early hours of Yom Kippur between
the Minister of Defence and the Chief of Staff, and during their
subsequent joint meeting with the Prime Minister, there was
tension, but certainly no undue worry. In both instances the atmosphere was businesslike as they discussed the extent to which the
reserves were to be called up. There was no dramatic confrontation
as was reported later orally and in writing in discussions of the

events of the war. Indeed the conference could not have been anything other than businesslike as it was not concerned with any particularly pressing question, given the estimate of the situation underlying the 'Iron Ram' war games according to which the regular army division in Sinai together with the air force would be able to halt the Egyptian attack. In any case, the reserve divisions were not meant to enter the battle before the third day of the war. Those responsible for the conduct of the war, the Defence Minister and the Chief of Staff representing the defence establishment, and the Prime Minister, joined by Ministers Yisrael Galili and Yigael Allon, civilian members of the government who also possessed military experience, were mainly concerned with the politics of the impending battle: issuing a warning to Egypt and Syria and refraining from steps, such as a pre-emptive air strike against Syria, which might have given the impression to the United States that Israel had initiated the hostilities. However, no one involved in the matter could have believed that it was possible to halt the two Arab war machines by issuing a warning or by offering assurances as to Israel's peaceful intentions: the Jordanian example in the Six Day War should have taught them that gestures of that kind had no military value. Nevertheless, Dayan has written that in view of what the government was told on the subject, it decided that issuing such an assurance might still be useful.

If, on the morning of Yom Kippur, those in charge of the war had time to engage in dubious speculation of this sort or to adapt their actions to the needs of making Israel's innocence more apparent for propaganda purposes, that is another indication that the political leadership was not unduly worried, further corroborating the supposition implied by forecasts about the war then current in the IDF and the government ('They start the war, we halt them, we hit them hard from the air, we destroy their missile batteries and artillery — then we go over to the offensive', in Dayan's words). Not only that; as Henry Kissinger relates in *Years of Upheaval*,[2] the messages that reached him from Israel were full of self-confidence up to the reversal on 12 October.

None the less, behind the mask of serenity and the illusions about an easy way out of the renewed military confrontation, the government which met to take decisions on the evening after the Yom Kippur fast was consumed by doubt and confused about the policies to be adopted towards the Arab states. The ministers knew full well that in Egypt voices had been raised in favour of coming to terms with Israel — and Egypt was recognised as setting the tone on the Arab side. The ministers viewed this development as confirmation of the doves' position that there might be an opening on the Arab side, and that Israel must bear some of the blame for the renewed war because of its intransigence. This view was held in particular by the ministers representing the views current in Israel before 1967, such as the Minister of Finance and the Foreign Minister. The Prime Minister, Golda Meir, was bound to be aware of these opinions, but she could not shake off the influence of hawks like the Defence Minister. However, Dayan himself was torn between two truths: in his heart of hearts he knew that Egypt would never agree to an indefinite IDF presence on the banks of the Suez Canal; but on the other hand he insisted on remaining in Sharm Al-Sheikh, in an offensive position across from the soft underbelly of Egypt. Beyond all this, the government was also aware of the political futility of military victory: Israel did not want additional territory, it knew the danger facing the IDF if it had to occupy the densely populated west bank of the Suez Canal, and it had certainly learned from experience that holding on to a territorial bargaining counter did not necessarily promote a political settlement.

It seems that this ambivalence among the key personalities and various groups of ministers was no less responsible for the development of an atmosphere of panic between 9 and 14 October than was the disappointment with the course of the battle or the dismay at Israeli losses of men and material. On 9 October Henry Kissinger concluded that Israel had suffered a strategic defeat in the wake of the counter-attack by two reserve divisions, a poorly co-ordinated operation in which many casualties were incurred and which was repulsed by the Egyptians. He also sensed the desperation beginning to pervade the country, notwithstanding the optimistic official reports. On that date he told the Israeli ambassador in Washington: 'Israel will have to pull itself together and overcome what is beginning to look like incipient chaos'. In fact, on 12 October Israel asked the United States to negotiate a cease-fire in place, resigning itself to the Egyptian gains.

It is not too fanciful to say that, had another government been in power at the time, the opening stages might have looked very different. The errors committed by the government of Golda Meir were elementary, although her cabinet included men with military experience and knowledge of international politics. She and her colleagues failed to understand that there was no contradiction between willingness to come to political terms as proposed by President Sadat and going to war in order to improve those terms, nor was she sufficiently sceptical about the advice she received from the high command of the IDF and the Ministry of Defence. In addition, there was the process of erosion to which the government, having been in power too long, was subject, and disagreement among its leading members on fundamentals: a tried and true recipe for military and psychological setbacks — the chaos of which Kissinger had spoken. Hence there is reason to believe that the subsequent events of the war — the military recovery, the passing to the counter-attack in the north and south, the crossing of the Suez Canal and the surrounding of the Egyptian Third Army — were largely due to the free hand given to the IDF. The ultimate course of the war was dictated by the operational commanders of a supremely effective war machine which rapidly adapted to a battlefield reality substantially different from that which it had expected. The political leadership tagged along behind the army rather than directing it and, lacking moral and spiritual resources, it was incapable of providing support and inspiration to the army in the field. In other words: the Yom Kippur War lacked the Moshe Dayan of the Six Day War. The man was still there, but his spiritual power had declined; he no longer inspired confidence or radiated leadership.

There is no satisfactory answer to the question of why the public did not settle accounts with the Labour government for the dangerous failures in its functioning during the Yom Kippur War and remove it in short order by voting for Gahal (the early version of the Likud). Some people attribute this failure to the powerful systemic shock from which the voters had not yet recovered between 24 October, the date of the ceasefire in the south, and 31 December 1973, election day. Moreover, since fighting continued in the north, the people may have been naturally reluctant to rock the boat. Other observers believe that it was the promise implicit in the convening of the Geneva Conference, an Arab-Israeli peace conference under joint US and Soviet chairmanship, based on Security Council Resolution 338, which persuaded the dwindling majority of voters to maintain their traditional loyalty to the coalition headed by the Labour Party, which favoured going to Geneva. Possibly both these causes were at work simultaneously. However, it quickly became apparent that peace, as the Israelis understood the word, was not in the offing, and the voters soon began to drift away from Labour. Deepening alienation from its rule was openly expressed by protest groups which surfaced and directed their fire particularly against Moshe Dayan. He was held to be chiefly responsible for the management of a war in which everything had taken place contrary to expectations, and following which it was clear that Israel would have to part with territorial bargaining assets which were supposed to be bartered for peace, without, however, receiving the peace it wanted in return. The broad outlines of partial settlements began to emerge in the negotiated separation of forces agreements in the north and the south. Israel had to give up a central article of its political faith, namely, that the IDF would not withdraw a single step except in return for peace. Golda Meir's government was now agreeing to withdraw from broad expanses of territory in return for merely observing the cease-fire — and everyone realised that this would be the pattern of the process developing from Henry Kissinger's shuttle diplomacy.

Thus the bankruptcy of the Labour Party's policy became clearly visible. It had previously enabled the party both to carry out the national agenda of territorial aggrandisement and to delude itself — and to delude the devotees of little Israel, pre–5 June 1967 vintage — with the hope that sooner or later Israel would free itself of the territories and return to business as usual on the pre-war pattern: building the economy and promoting social welfare. It was the bankruptcy of that policy no less than the Agranat Commission Report, that forced Prime Minister Golda Meir to resign and to abandon hope of re-establishing the government with Moshe Dayan as Minister of Defence.

The new Cabinet installed by the Labour Party bore the imprint of four men, Yitzhak Rabin, Shimon Peres, Yigael Allon, and Yehoshua Rabinowitz, new faces at that level of government. Although warmly greeted by the public, within a short time it became clear that the new government suffered from the same split personality that had crippled all Labour governments since the Six Day War. The national agenda centred around borders, and territorial expansion, and whatever followed from these priorities was never acceptable to many of its leaders. In order to stay in power, the Labour leadership had previously reconciled itself to the current political fashion and granted its prophet, Moshe Dayan, a position and authority which he deserved neither by virtue of his standing in the party hierarchy, on the one hand, nor as a reward for his heretical views, on the other. Nevertheless, Dayan's removal did not solve the problem either, because, after the end of the Yom

Kippur War, circumstances dictated the liquidation of the legacy of the Six Day War. Willingly or not, the government remained preoccupied, under heavy pressure from friends and foes alike, with the issue of the borders. Since it was guided by a national agenda whose principal goal, even after the war, was to retain as much territory as possible under Israel's control, it invested the greater part of its efforts in striving towards that goal, despite a continuously worsening international climate. The alternative, namely to conclude that the war left the Arab states no choice other than to reconcile themselves, if only *de facto*, to Israel's continued existence in their midst, and that, in consequence, it was possible to return to the old national agenda, remembered from the great decade of Mapai between 1949 and 1959, was not even considered. Perhaps the objective conditions for such a change of course were not yet ripe. At any rate, the government concentrated its energies on finding a solution to the issue of territories and borders, although three of its four key men, the Prime Minister and his Foreign and Defence Ministers, were divided between their desire to retain as much territory as possible, as befitted the national agenda, and the inner urge to free the country of the 1967 war and the burden of its heritage.

The international community had wasted a lot of time and effort up to then, and has continued to do so ever since, in reproaching Israel for holding on to the conquered territories. One could speculate as to what might have been achieved if a mere fraction of that effort had instead been invested in urging the Arabs to do something practical about their vague notions of reconciling themselves to the existence of Israel. One could also imagine the direction events might have taken if President Sadat had gone to Israel while the Rabin government was in power. In that case the government and the public would probably have been able to rid themselves of the demon of borders and territories and to concentrate on a national programme with a different character from that which had guided the country since 1967. The Rabin government was tireless but had no luck at all. Nevertheless it never threw up the sponge: in the incessant turmoil between one of Henry Kissinger's nerve-racking visits and the next, the government not only carried on with its task of restraining inflation and staunching the outflow of foreign exchange, but also managed to reform the tax system and introduced a value added tax, steps which previous, more powerful governments had not dared to take.

These reforms indicate the residual presence of the pre-war (Mapai) component in the government's repertory of ideas, which had survived during the ascendancy of the national agenda focused on borders and territories. Moreover, until 1977, the election year, the economic leadership under Yehoshua Rabinowitz, a veteran member of Mapai, never ceased talking economic sense to the public, or demanding sacrifices in order to improve the economic situation. However, the dichotomy — territory versus economic and social reform — laid bare the seams holding together the two elements in Labour: those who accepted the 1967 version of the national agenda, and those who remained true to the old faith of the past decades. These seams were never very strong, and they ripped apart under the combined pressure of external and internal events.

Cases of corruption were uncovered right and left during the Rabin administration, hastening its disintegration. Corruption was far from unknown in Israel: it had been imported both from Eastern Europe and the Middle East. However, its main cause lay in the influx of large, uncontrolled funds: when bureaucracies are called upon to distribute enormous sums of money, some of it inevitably sticks to the fingers of the people handing it out. But now a new, previously unknown or at least unpublicised kind of corruption came to light. The people chiefly implicated were members of the political elite: for example, Michael Tsur, one of Pinhas Sapir's closest assistants before his appointment as head of a large private corporation, and, even more so, Asher Yadlin, another of Sapir's trusted associates and a central figure in the Histadrut economic organisation, who was just about to be appointed Governor of the Bank of Israel. The death blow to the public's confidence in the integrity of its political elite came with the rumours of bribery, which were never proved, associated with the Housing Minister, Avraham Ofer, who subsequently took his own life. The matter of Prime Minister Rabin's legally questionable dollar account probably did little harm to the party, for one cannot damage what has already been destroyed.

At this time a new party came into being, the Democratic Movement for Change, with a political programme based on the desire to clean up society and rid the government of corruption. The movement was really a pressure group disguised as a political party, but before shattering to bits, it managed to attract many former Labour supporters, thus hastening Labour's downfall.

•

Notes

1. He was later Israel's Ambassador to the United States and Prime Minister, 1974–7.

2. Henry Kissinger, *Years of Upheaval* (Little Brown and Co., Boston, Toronto, 1982).

4   CHALLENGE AND CONQUEST

The turn-round of 1977 was late in arriving. Some time between 1960 and 1965 the coalition led by Mapai had exhausted the voters' patience, having worn out its political substance and accomplished the national agenda with which it was identified. In the following years it was stopped in its programmatic tracks and had to deal with matters to which it was unaccustomed, and which it found distasteful. But it kept its head above water by means of its will to survive, by adapting itself to the new winds which had begun to blow in Israeli society, and by using the knowledge and experience in government which the party and its representatives had garnered during its many years of leadership in Jewish Palestine and Israel.

Its political skill was especially evident in the period between the Six Day War and the Yom Kippur War, in its adoption of Moshe Dayan, who at that time was a national hero, pioneering the formation of a new national agenda. It was helpful to the party that Dayan, for sentimental reasons and because of his background, was willing to hitch himself to its wagon, although the squeak of its rusty axles was audible from afar. He himself had never been one to build up political power, preferring to let others work to mobilise the political power he needed to accomplish what he had at heart — tracing out new borders and forging the conditions necessary for practical co-existence between the Jewish administration and its Arab subjects within the Land of Israel. For, as he said, 'The highest goal is to make the new territories into Israeli territories.' In order to retain power and enjoy its fruits, the Labour Party not only reconciled itself to the constraints of implementing this national agenda, but also to the acceptance of political values alien to a significant portion of its supporters. It even went so far as to include Dayan's comrades from the Rafi faction within the front rank of its leaders.

Economic Infrastructure

Mapai, later the Labour Party, had already come to the end of the line politically in the early 1960s. It had also given the economy a structure foreign to its elitist conceptions. Later on we shall discuss the outlines of the party's economic policy in some detail; what must be said here is that the man who increasingly made his mark on economic thought and activity, Pinhas Sapir, understood that his main task was to provide employment for a growing population. When he was appointed Minister of Commerce and Industry in 1955 he took it upon himself to provide jobs in manufacturing, recognising that the process of absorption in agriculture had reached its limits — in no small measure because of the restrictions imposed on its further development by limited water supplies. Sapir achieved a historic success: people had jobs and were working for a living, for better or worse, and thus a primary tenet, in the Labour Zionist creed was implemented — the turning of untrained people, in most cases unaccustomed to physical labour, into operatives in farming, construction or manufacturing — what for want of a more elegant phrase we shall call 'productivisation'. In the process of its implementation, Sapir sought the assistance of those who, for lack of a more precise term, must be called entrepreneurs. Most of them were men blessed with a talent for locating public funds buried in the small print of budget documents. Once found, they proposed to the various ministries the use of such funds for the setting up of industrial plant, offering employment to a certain number of people and commensurate profit for themselves. The preference for entrepreneurs of this sort, rather than bureaucratic initiative, on the part of a government called socialist by its rivals and critics — and which also saw itself in that light — is indicative of Pinhas Sapir's ideological outlook, and in fact that of Mapai in general. The result was predictable: under Mapai rule, thanks to the largesse of the 'number one patron', Pinhas Sapir, an entrepreneurial class began to grow and prosper; it also sought to justify the economic advantages it enjoyed by increasing business efficiency, by improving the quality of its products, by increasing competitive ability in export markets, and so on. To achieve these ends it borrowed freely from concepts taken from another social ethos, best called entrepreneurial, and foreign to Israel, which had previously clung to egalitarian pioneering values. Some time during the 1960s Pinhas Sapir's entrepreneurs succeeded, largely with the support of academics and media people who viewed this social development with favour, in imposing their concepts and values on Israeli society. Under their influence the economy changed from a system aiming at the maximisation of employment and as egalitarian an income distribution as possible, to a system in which the guiding principles were efficiency and profitability. In other words, the economic policy of Mapai, i.e. Sapir, lent the economy a decidedly entrepreneurial cast.

In the mid-1960s therefore the economic infrastructure was ready and waiting for a new national agenda compatible with its entrepreneurial character, as demanded by the economic creed of the General Zionist element of Gahal and also of the 'bourgeois' component of the Herut party. The Six Day War and its aftermath added the practical elements needed to make the nationalist, expansionist national agenda a realistic one. It also seemed that an organisational alternative to Mapai had emerged: Gahal, established in early 1965, became a force around which an alternative government could coalesce. Why then was there no change in government? A partial answer to this question has been offered earlier in this book, but that answer is less than satisfactory. It is indeed hard to explain, let alone justify in retrospect, the continued survival of a regime that had little new to offer and whose energies exhausted themselves in the day-to-day operation of the machinery of government. One might add here that it is unfortunate that the Labour regime outlived its usefulness. It is doubtful whether the evils that befell Israel in the Yom Kippur War would have happened under a government more alert to the danger of Arab attack: and, to give the hypothetical Likud government the benefit of the doubt, it might have been more willing to question the conventional military wisdom, something which the Meir-Dayan government lacked the moral courage to do.

The International Dimension

It is possible that the reason for the survival of the Mapai-Labour government and the delay in the Likud's rise to power should be sought beyond Israel's borders and also in the way the reactions of the outside world to the protracted struggle in the Middle East were perceived in Israel. The Labour party, which was basically isolationist and inward-looking, was also understood to favour a friendly attitude to the gentile world and a willingness to communicate with it on the basis of its values at a time when liberalism and social democracy were in the ascendant. As long as the world reciprocated with sympathy and warmth — the victory in the Six Day War brought a feast of love for Israel — the mutual approval served as a justification for the Labour government, which was known to be committed to the maintenance of such a policy.

But the Yom Kippur War found a world out of patience with Israel; in the western media the Arab attack was reported with jubilation, and US efforts to resupply Israel during the war encountered obstacles, even to the extent that West Germany, then regarded as wholly subservient to the United States, mustered the courage to refuse to allow the use of US airbases on German territory to refuel the cargo planes flying in emergency supplies for the IDF. Then came the oil crisis, and with it the West's discovery of 'Arab rights'; and even before the Arab attack, the African states — admittedly not in the first division internationally — broke off diplomatic relations with Israel. There was also the campaign of vilification in the United Nations, which struck the Israeli public like a bolt from the blue. The climax of this campaign was the passage on 11 November 1975 of the resolution against Zionism, which was termed racist, by a large majority in the UN General Assembly. The picture of a pistol-packing Yasser Arafat, speaking from the podium of the General Assembly and receiving a standing ovation from the delegates, utterly destroyed the Israeli public's faith in international co-operation and the usefulness of maintaining a friendly dialogue with other countries. As a result, Israelis lost confidence in the government and the party identified with this policy. Menachem Begin's Likud promised to change Israel's relations with the rest of the world and to put them on a basis of confrontation, in which the most determined would triumph. This contributed to his rise to power.

It has been noted earlier that, when the Likud took power in 1977, it was not called upon to innovate. The substantive change in policy, namely the replacement of the Mapai national agenda of the first decade of the state, best summed up as 'a little Israel minding its own business', had already taken place ten years before Menachem Begin was sworn in as Prime Minister. But although the Likud did not innovate, it did refine and concentrate the issues, leaving no room for obscurity and the misunderstandings that blurred the first version of the greater Israel.

An editorial in *Haaretz* the day after the 1977 elections described the change, which had placed the Likud at the centre of a ruling coalition in place of Labour, as follows: 'Instead of a policy of political agreements which is perceived . . . as a policy of unilateral withdrawal . . . a large number, possibly the majority, of Israel's citizens want a firmer posture towards the outside world'. Labour was displaced because the general public believed that it and its government had reached the end of the road, not only from a programmatic point of view but also functionally: the signs of disintegration, moral, political, and organisational, were too apparent and too numerous to be ignored. However, the public did not vote for the Democratic Movement for Change, but for the Likud, because it wanted a more straight-backed posture vis-á-vis the gentiles — not only the Arabs — and the coalition headed by Menachem Begin looked like promising precisely this. And the public was not disappointed: the upheavel of 1977 led to a significant change in Israel's relations with the rest of the world, the outcome of a deliberate effort with which the new Prime Minister must be credited, or, as the case may be, blamed.

Menachem Begin was assisted by a historic development. The war in Vietnam and the energy crisis considerably weakened the position of the United States in the world, and this did not pass unnoticed in the Middle East, where, from Israel's point of view, the US had played the role of global policeman, responsible for law and order, the arbitrator and umpire in local disputes. The Vietnam War revealed the United States as harbouring imperialist ambitions without imperial firmness. In other words, it was not prepared to make the sacrifices necessary to achieve its ambitions to impose settlements and to appoint rulers according to its understanding of its own national interest. However, it was still strong enough to bring pressure to bear on Israel to adopt certain policies, inasmuch as the rest of the world was on the American side. Having perceived these fundamental facts, Begin then took the first of the four basic decisions which marked his period of rule. This was the decision to seek agreement with Egypt so as to achieve room to manoeuvre in order to strengthen Israeli rule over the entire Land of Israel, up to the Jordan. In this he acted like a chess player who sacrifices a knight to gain a better position for his queen. President Sadat's initiative, generally regarded, and not without reason, as the action which altered the whole course of events in the region, took place at an opportune time from Begin's point of view, and while others were still concerned with preparations for the first meeting between the Egyptians and Israelis after Sadat's visit to Jerusalem, which was to take place in the Egyptian town of Ismailia, he rushed to

Washington with an autonomy plan which he himself had drafted, in order to prepare the ground for the exchange he had in mind.

At this point it is proper to clarify the difference between Begin's model and Dayan's earlier one, of a national agenda based on expanding Israel's borders. Dayan's image of Israel included a stronghold on the Gulf of Suez as well as military rule over the Land of Israel, but without interference in the daily life of the Arab population. In contrast, Begin never saw the Sinai or any part of it as territory vital to Israel: he was prepared to fight for the maintenance of an Israeli presence in Sinai, but for a dual purpose. He wanted to show his own people, and the rest of the world, that Israel had stopped making easy concessions, and that anyone who wanted to obtain something from Israel would have to pay the full price for it. The question of whether or not he was right in estimating that, for Israel's peace and security, occupation of the Land of Israel up to the Jordan was preferable to a strong presence in Sinai, is still being debated in the political community. However, from his point of view, this question simply never arose. There were several reasons for this. The issue of the legal status of the Land of Israel is still open, while that of Sinai is closed, in that the peninsula has been an acknowledged part of Egypt since the beginning of the century. Further, if the Sinai is demilitarised, the threat on the southern border seems less than that on the eastern border, which is much closer to the heart of Israel. Above all (and the Prime Minister's reasons are presented here in ascending order of importance), Begin came to power essentially because of his faith, which had hardly been eroded since the day he first entered Israeli politics, in the historical, even the divine, right of the Jewish people to the land of its fathers, at least as far east as the Jordan. Therefore, when he realised that he could not have both Dayan's outpost at the southern tip of Sinai and the Land of Israel, he unhesitatingly chose to sacrifice the Sinai in order to win the Land of Israel. It should be noted here that the momentous alliance between Begin and Ariel Sharon (Minister of Agriculture in the first Begin Government) was struck at this point: Sharon was the man to whom the Prime Minister telephoned at a critical moment in the negotiations with Presidents Sadat and Carter at Camp David, in order to get his approval for relinquishing the Sinai Peninsula, including its military air bases and the civilian settlements there. Sharon gave his blessing, thus putting the Prime Minister in his debt, and he repeatedly drew against that credit until it was exhausted with the massacres at Sabra and Shatila.

Begin's underlying model for the agreement with Egypt was never in doubt. On the one hand, he followed the general rule laid down by his predecessor, Yitzhak Rabin, who had held that it was possible to come to a separate agreement with Egypt. On the other hand, he was guided by his intuitive sense of the limits of American power, expressed in the United States' unwillingness to impose a comprehensive settlement on the area, although it wanted one. He also believed it was possible to make a deal with Sadat that would give Sinai to the Egyptians and Palestine to Israel. The recurrent crises marring the peace talks in the period between Sadat's visit to Jerusalem and the signing of the treaty in the White House, about a year and a half later, occurred because of the firm position taken by the Prime Minister: he insisted on a full recompense to Israel in return for giving up Sinai. Begin never considered any change in the formula, 'Leave me something in Sinai and I will make things easier for you in Palestine'. His conception of the essence of the deal with Egypt was absolutely straightforward: just as Sadat insisted that he would not concede 'a single inch', so Begin held fast to his position. His concessions with regard to the text of the Israeli-Egyptian peace treaty were merely verbal, and the treaty was never intended to be amenable to a loose interpretation.

Perhaps this is the place to note that Begin's speeches extolling peace, his main argument in support of the peace treaty with Egypt, enhanced his status among the general public in Israel. Along with their idea of Israel as a regional power and with their desire to give the gentiles their come-uppance for their hostile and insulting attitude towards Israel, the people also longed for peace. But Begin, despite what he said — which more than once aroused suspicions that a sworn pacifist stood at the head of the Likud government, heralding once again the prophetic vision of eternal peace — remained true to himself: a social Darwinist, a man who could bear witness, on the strength of the horrors visited upon himself and his family, that force was preferable to moral superiority. The seven years of his rule as Prime Minister go to prove this: he took Esau's blessing for Israel, 'By the sword thou shalt live'.

The Settlement Policy

However, at the same time as he decided to abandon the idea of maximal expansion of Israel's borders and to concentrate on laying the formal foundation for Israeli rule over western Palestine, including the achievement of international recognition as conferred by the peace treaty with Egypt, Begin also made another decision with regard to the method for actually imposing Israeli rule. He chose, in prima facie surprising fashion, the method of settlements. What was surprising about this decision was its deviation from Jabotinsky's[1] revisionist ideology. The position of the revisionist movement with regard to land settlement varied between lack of interest and condemnation for two main reasons. One of them is presented by the historian of the movement. Dr Yakov Shavit:[2]

> From the time of its first founding in the middle twenties until the middle thirties, *and also afterwards*, the social composition and political structure of revisionism did not permit constructive land settlement. . . . The leaders of the movement in Europe naturally could not be involved in settlement, *nor did they wish to be*. (italics added)

Along with the objective circumstances of the time and the personal tendencies deriving from them, their basic political idea of the way to take control of the country also played a role in the revisionists' indifference and negative attitude towards land settlement. Jabotinsky's followers believed that the only immediate task incumbent upon Zionism was the establishment of Jewish *sovereignty* in the country: hence their emphasis on the need to create a Jewish military force and to achieve the appropriate understandings with the mandatory power. Settlement in various parts of Palestine seemed of secondary importance to them, a wasted effort, something that would follow upon seizing power, which was their first priority. In this the Jabotinsky school differed from its Labour rival, whose method was to achieve Jewish control over Palestine based on the purchase of land and settlement on it: parcel by parcel, acre by acre.

Dayan's concept, based on the imposition of military control over Judea, Samaria, and the Gaza Strip and excluding Jewish settlement in areas heavily populated by Arabs, was thus the legitimate descendant of Jabotinsky principles. Moreover, it was in harmony with the declared tenet of the revisionist movement, namely, that the Arabs were to be citizens with equal rights under Jewish sovereignty. This principle implied that they were entitled to a sufficient reserve of land to absorb the Arab population, assuming that they would not wish or be able to settle in the midst of the Jewish population. Dayan's position implied that a state in which two nations lived side by side, a bi-national state, which logically should have been acceptable to him as well as to all of Jabotinsky's disciples, could not exist in peace, unless friction between the two alien ethnic components were prevented. However, Begin adopted the method of massive land settlement in the midst of the Arab inhabitants as a means of imposing Israeli control over all of western Palestine.

Such a substantial deviation from Jabotinsky's views would hardly have been feasible, if a body which was not part of the Likud organisation had not come forward to implement Begin's settlement policy. This organisation, Gush Emunim (The Bloc of the Faithful), was not the one which decided upon the policy; rather it was Begin who perceived that the Bloc would be a useful tool to implement it, and already some time before the 1977 elections he had decided to make use of it. On 20 May 1977 the future Prime Minister went to a temporary encampment of Gush Emunim in Kadum to take part in celebrations over the arrival of a Torah Scroll, and in a short speech he promised that there would be many more new settlements. In making this promise he was not shooting from the hip (in general it should be remembered that Begin was not one to shoot from the hip) but giving well-considered advance notice of policies that would be executed. And he did in fact execute them. The peace treaty with Egypt and the concessions in the autonomy plan which were wrung from him by joint efforts of the Egyptians and the Americans made the Prime Minister regard it as even more pressing to hasten and expand the settlement effort because of doubts about the permanence of the Israeli military presence in Judea, Samaria, and the Gaza Strip. In other words, Begin, the disciple of Jabotsinky, came to adopt the classic Labour Movement doctrine of conquest through land settlement, thus launching one of the more conspicuous changes of the past decade. This course of action, quite apart from its political effects, forged another link in the alliance between Menachem Begin and Ariel Sharon, the champion of the conquest of the Land of Israel by means of populating it with Jews. Sharon was Gush Emunim's man in the government and a past disciple — not surprisingly — of the Palestine Workers' Party, Mapai.

Before inspecting Gush Emunim more closely, let us briefly sum

up the political balance-sheet with regard to Begin's second fundamental decision. Along with the clear advantage, from his point of
view, of a highly visible defiance of world opinion, it strengthened
Israel's claim to permanent ownership of the whole of the Land of
Israel, in terms of population. However, he paid a stiff price in
rousing the Arab population from its dormant state since the 1967
defeat and provoking acts of violent resistance; he tacitly
encouraged some settlers to resist the civil authority and to launch
acts of counter-terror against the Arabs. He also polarised the
nation; it should be recalled that the resignation of two of his senior
ministers, Moshe Dayan and Ezer Weitzmann, was a direct or
indirect outcome of this decision. Thus if ever there was a union of
opposites, the curse of a blessing, that phrase certainly applies to
Begin's decision to abandon his revisionist faith and to convert to
that of the Labour Movement, by adopting their method of
imposing Israeli rule on the whole Land of Israel.

Gush Emunim

Gush Emunim is a powerful expression of the frustration and
resentment aroused among orthodox Jews by the secular environment. It is not the only such expression, but it was singularly suited
to the national agenda which began to guide the state after 1967,
centred upon expanding Israel's borders. It is noteworthy that the
issue was territorial expansion in general, not merely control of the
Land of Israel. The first demonstration by Gush Emunim, in 1974,
was directed against the IDF withdrawal from the western, African
bank of the Suez Canal. Again, a bitter battle was waged by Gush
Emunim against the withdrawal from the Yamit region although
that town, just south of the international frontier with Egypt, has no
historical connection with the land of the patriarchs which,
according to Rabbi Yehuda Kook, in his tract, 'Thou Shalt Not
Fear', it is forbidden to return to the gentiles. Thus Gush Emunim is
not a religious version of the Society for the Land of Israel,[3] but a
body which sanctifies every conquest, no matter where. What
distinguishes it from other expansionists is that it uses quotations
from Scripture, the Talmud, and Rabbinic commentators in order
to justify its expansionist ideology, which is essentially pagan.

In his 'Gush Anthem', the poet Yitzhak Laor brought out the
sources of that frustration and resentment:

> We are the knitted skullcaps. No one calls us religious jerks any
> more.
> They don't pull our hair fringes, they don't kick us out of the
> neighbourhood
> Games. They don't call us baby rabbis, for we are soldiers
> In the army of the Lord of Hosts, the Israeli Defence Force, and
> we take revenge
> For everything they did to us here in the land of our exile, for all
> the lies they told about us, for all
> They accused us of falsely, killed us, persecuted us, and laughed
> at us . . .

Now it happens that Yitzhak Laor is not an orthodox Jew, and it is
unlikely that he has personally experienced what orthodox Jews go
through, particularly orthodox Jewish children. But with his artistic
talent he was able to portray the inner experience of such people
with marvellous accuracy. The world of orthodox Jews is subject to
constant tension between the obligation to resist a world full of
hostility and temptations and remain within the four confines of a
way of life based on the 613 commandments of the Jewish law, and
the impulse to succumb to temptation, to become involved, even to
become a leader, if only to teach errant people to live according to
the Torah.

The strong urge to break out of the walls of the ghetto of the
believers and into the Jewish ghetto surrounding it, is not peculiar to
Israel, although the continued existence of the ghetto within an
independent Jewish society is unique. While secular Jews have
achieved national redemption through the State of Israel, that
redemption has neither reached the orthodox nor affected them. To
this the orthodox community has reacted in various ways: by
denying the redemptive pretensions of the secular Jewish state,
along with a quiet but stubborn effort to win back those who are ripe
for religion; or, alternatively, by joining in those actions of the
secular Jews which fit in with the religious tradition, initiating
contact at points of proximity with those who dwell beyond the walls
of the religious ghetto.

The latter was the path taken by the National Religious Party and
the synagogues, houses of prayer, and the *yeshivot* (rabbinical
colleges) under their patronage. The community which they served
reconciled itself to the secular state and apparently to the leading
role played by the secular elite in the life of that state. The NRP

segment of orthodox Jewry limited its demands to the particular needs of its community (the sabbath, *kashrut*, laws governing personal status, etc.). The secular leaders of the state were prepared to respond generously to these demands. The arrangement, which became institutionalised in the course of time under the name 'The Historic Alliance between the Labour Movement and the Mizrachi' (the forerunner of the NRP), did not change the reality of the ghetto, which derived from the self-segregation of a community which could not, because of the obligations and prohibitions of the Torah, act according to the values of a modern secular society. The religious public remained a minority, one that felt different; the orthodox also experienced frustration deriving from their inability to live like everyone around them and from being denied advancement within the secular society on equal terms — a denial which was felt especially in public life. The sense of being excluded did not bring peace even to those who identified wholeheartedly with the national goals of the secular state, until a substantial change occurred in the secular camp which permitted the orthodox to widen the breach in the walls of their ghetto.

This change originated in the disappointment, which was not peculiar to Israel, with welfare democracy and the affluent society which, in one form or another, had dominated the West, including Israel, since the end of the Second World War. People discovered that social equality entailed the bureaucratisation of life and the loss of solidarity based on shared hardship. As for material plenty, it was also found to be a mixed blessing. For example, the slogan 'A Car for Every Worker' fired the imagination, but its implementation produced unbearable air pollution and traffic jams which turned the use of private automobiles into a nightmare. In the Western world, of which Israel is a part, doubts have arisen as to the blessings of egalitarianism and its influence. In the 1970s these doubts were strengthened by economic difficulties, mass unemployment, and decline in real incomes, a phenomenon unknown and unexpected since the 1950s. Events within Israel only exacerbated the feeling of disappointment: one war opened up a path leading the Jewish people to its ancient past, but a second war and its aftermath returned it to the reality of the existential fears which had pursued it throughout the centuries of exile. The veteran leadership disappointed the country, in that the material paradise it offered proved to be both unstable and subject to dangers from within and without. In these circumstances it is no wonder that, increasingly, people yearned for the stable values of religion and tradition, the land and the Bible. In the 1970s secular Israel was prepared to heed new messages, even if the 'new' was in fact as ancient as the people itself. The encounter with religion in an aggressive, nationalistic guise was natural and unforced. The heads of *Yeshivas* and their students in the NRP were not mistaken when they began to discern the signals of redemption, not only in the broad national sense, but also in the sense of redeeming the orthodox community from its isolation within its cultural and social ghetto.

Nor was it all talk; they were ready to act. Gush Emunim, which grew up and organised itself within the NRP *yeshivas*, was an instrument in the hands of its teachers and rabbis with which to breach the walls of the ghetto and meet with the secular community which had become receptive to messages invested with the venerable and sacred authority of the Torah. Moreover, this time the orthodox set out on an equal footing with the secular majority: Gush Emunim was created to march in the van, and it carried out the task assigned to it by its teachers. It assisted in the campaign to discredit the Labour leadership which had remained loyal to the values and national agenda of the 1950s. It helped Menachem Begin and his companions prove the nation's vitality by challenging the outside world, the gentiles, who doubt the right of the Jewish state to exist, and it set forth to carry out the Biblical commandment, 'and thou shalt inherit it', with reference to the entire Land of Israel. The spiritual leaders of Gush Emunim, NRP politicians like Zevulon Hammer, and secular Jews on its fringes like Ariel Sharon, who had close links with it, had the right to expect that the Gush would lift them to the pinnacles of power, thus doing away once and for all with the handicaps hampering religious politicians. In the past they had been limited to begging for budgetary allocations for their *yeshivas*, but kept at a distance from the highest levels of government. This was no longer to be the case.

Much has been said of the burning idealism motivating members of Gush Emunim — a virtue which, even among the non-orthodox, invested them with the aura of the pioneering settlers of the 1920s and 1930s. However, closer inspection of their beliefs reveals an ideological uni-dimensionality: once the element of nationalism is removed, the body is left without a soul.

The difference is evident if one compares today's West Bank settlements — emanations of Gush Emunim's central doctrine — with the settlements of the 1920s and 1930s. At that time too the settlers saw themselves as emissaries of the people, but they undertook to satisfy additional ideological demands, which took more than just settling the land to fulfil. They took it upon themselves to pioneer a unique way of life which would stand a prolonged economic test; a settlement which could not support itself over time, was regarded by its members, as well as by the people around them, as a failure. The two forms of co-operative agricultural settlement, the *kibbutz* and the *moshav*, therefore served more than one purpose: they expanded the geographical area of Jewish settlement, they contributed to the health of Jewish society (by reversing its inverted occupational pyramid), and they increased (at any rate, they were meant to increase) the economic self-sufficiency of the *Yishuv*. Above and beyond all that, they created a unique pattern of social organisation. The settlements of Gush Emunim do not have ambitions of that sort: they are 'community' settlements with no more positive social content than an urban co-operative apartment house in a neighbourhood with a higher than average rate of violent crime. Clearly such a bond is insufficient to assure prolonged communal life. There is less likelihood than in the case of the early settlements that the Gush Emunim settlers will remain cohesive, for they are bound together only by the thread of nationalism.

Along with ideological poverty in the secular realm, the situation of the Gush is also tenuous from the religious point of view. In his book on Gush Emunim,[4] Tsvi Raanan quotes a conversation with a member of the secular Kibbutz Meuchad movement, now an activist in the nationalist Tehiya party, who was enthralled by the charms of Gush Emunim. He said, 'I told them in a discussion, . . . I'm much more extreme than you when it comes to the Land of Israel, because I can't be sure the Third Temple [i.e., the modern State of Israel] won't be destroyed. You have an alternative. If, perish the thought, the Third Temple actually is destroyed, you believe that the business will carry on'. Apart from his faulty logic, the speaker was also wrong with regard to the religious survival of the Gush. True, 'the business will carry on' from the point of view of Jews like those in the ultra-orthodox neighbourhood of Meah Shearim in Jerusalem or in Bnei Brak, gathered at the opposite pole of orthodox Jewish life. From their point of view the 'destruction of the Third Temple' would simply reveal the Sabbatean[5] nature of Gush Emunim. However, the teachers of Gush Emunim hold that the people of Israel are already living at the time of the advent of the

Messiah, and that, on the divine timetable, the countdown towards redemption has already begun. Redemption has clear criteria in the Jewish tradition. From the point of view of the traditional, if the Third Temple is destroyed, the 'business' is over. Gush Emunim will be swallowed up in the shadowy limbo of religions, exactly like the representative of Tehiya whose secular world was destroyed.

Judaism is for the tough-minded, not for the squeamish. Turning the other cheek is a late invention, never assimilated by the faith. Thus Gush Emunim is no exception: Rabbi Levinger and his flock flaunting Kalatchinkov submachine guns in Hebron fit easily into the spiritual landscape of the community they claim to represent. To be fair to it, the violence of Gush Emunim is all-embracing: both Jews and Arabs have suffered its blows.

In the meantime, the crime of the attack against the mayors of Nablus, Ramalla, and Al-Bireh has been purged, vindicating those who always claimed that a concerted effort and the investigative methods generally employed in such cases would discover the perpetrators among the settlers in the West Bank. But strong-arm methods were used against Jews as well, few of us will forget the battle for Yamit. It was waged without fire arms, but the term 'battle' is appropriate for the ardour and tenacity of the violent struggle waged by members of Gush Emunim against the army which came to evacuate them from Yamit. It was only blind chance that prevented severe physical casualties, even death, among the soldiers. Gush Emunim, as we said, maintains the tough-minded tradition of the Jewish people.

Some people are of the opinion that the violence accompanying public struggles in Israel is the particular contribution of the Oriental Jews, who brought with them in their baggage, it is said, the customs common in the Arab world. For instance, the people who broke up Labour Party rallies during the 1981 elections screaming 'Begin, Begin' were mostly Oriental Jews. However, they had predecessors who were born in Israel, and, in fact, even earlier, in the courts of the various Hassidic Rabbis in Eastern Europe, where it was accepted practice to stone members of rival courts and secular Jews. Young men wearing the long black coats of the ultra-orthodox or the knitted skullcaps of the NRP youth movement were the true setters of precedent, against which the amateurish howling of a few rowdies at Labour Party rallies pales into insignificance.

The star of Gush Emunim, which rose at a dizzy speed during the troubled times after the Yom Kippur War, now shows signs of waning. The Gush reached its zenith under the first Begin Government, when it took it upon itself to be the chief executor of the policy of populating Judea, Samaria and the Gaza Strip. Now it is no longer needed; and has been put aside because of a change in the task in hand. Nevertheless, there is no doubt that Gush Emunim was an outstanding feature of the period during which Menachem Begin was in charge of the implementation of the national agenda. It arose out of confusion and loss of direction, and at its end it faces a blank wall of disappointment; but it is an authentic Israeli and Jewish phenomenon whose roots penetrate far down into the soul of the people.

Action Against the PLO

As noted above, Menachem Begin's first decision on taking power was to create the international legal background for the entrenchment of Israeli rule over Judea, Samaria, and the Gaza Strip; to that end he strove for a separate peace with Egypt. His second decision, made at the same time, concerned the method for exercising that control. He chose, perhaps because the path of formal annexation was blocked, the method of land settlement, following the model created by the Labour Movement, which he detested. In both decisions he was assisted by Ariel Sharon, first, in authorising the abandonment of Sinai and second, in organising and fostering the settlement campaign of Gush Emunim in the eastern regions of the Land of Israel and in the Gaza Strip. When, in 1981, he was re-elected as Prime Minister, he saw that the time was ripe to settle accounts, his own and those of Israel, with the other claimant upon Palestine, the PLO.

People still wonder why he chose to make war, although he took care to disguise it as a form of police action which would last only a few days. The question is apt, given the nature of the PLO's threat to Israel and the assessment of the danger it posed. According to some people, the PLO problem is a political one, and cannot therefore be solved by military means. However this sounds like quibbling rather than facing up to facts. Begin may have been within his rights in viewing the military actions taken by the PLO — incursions into Israel for the purpose of committing highly visible acts of terrorism or attacking people or other targets abroad — as the foundation upon which the Palestinian organisation had built up its international position. If Israel were to destroy its military bases in Lebanon, the PLO would no longer be able to point to the various acts of the Palestinian guerrilla groups as reminders to the world that their resistance was still alive. If Israel succeeded in destroying the bases themselves, then the Arabs in Palestine and the Arab states which subsidise the PLO would cease to provide moral and financial support. As for the rest of the world, it regarded the PLO leadership as a kind of Palestinian government in exile, which was close to achieving its goals; it too would follow the Arab example. For that matter, Menachem Begin never took the view, and rightly so, that force cannot solve political problems; for he had seen with his own eyes how force had destroyed the state in which he was born and brought up, and how it had literally annihilated the ethnic basis on which he had hoped to establish the sovereign Jewish state in the Land of Israel.

One must not attribute the plan to go to war in Lebanon to these considerations alone. (Like most clever politicians, Begin often tried to kill as many birds as possible with one stone.) Thus, for example, according to a report in the special supplement published by the daily paper *Maariv* on 3 June 1983, the first anniversary of Operation Peace for the Galilee, the Prime Minister had proposed to his Cabinet colleagues that Israel should go to war in reprisal for the world's unanimous rejection of Israeli annexation of the Golan. The report further states that he had considered going to war in Lebanon as early as March 1982 in order to test Egyptian intentions and their commitment to the peace treaty with Israel. What was not reported, though it seems probable, is that the initiators of the proposal, the Defence Minister, Ariel Sharon, and the Chief of Staff, Rapahael Eitan (who depended on the support of the Prime Minister, as *Maariv* comments), planned to help Begin in his efforts to wipe out the depressing impression left in the public mind, especially among Likud supporters, by the evacuation from Sinai, including the military airfields and the settlements in the Yamit region. A victory over the PLO seemed to be tailor-made for that purpose.

One way or another, Begin could depend on his alliance with Sharon. He knew from experience that there were opponents within the Cabinet to a large-scale military action in Lebanon, and that, in order to stifle that opposition, he needed allies. Ariel Sharon had proved himself a faithful and effective ally both in authorising the withdrawal from Sinai and in implementing the policy of settling Judea, Samaria, and the Gaza Strip. Even though Begin, while doubling as Minister of Defence from 1979 until the elections of 1981, had suffered from Sharon's aggressive and insulting criticisms (at the time he described Sharon privately as a great general but a vicious person), he reckoned that Sharon would outweigh all the other hesitant ministers in the government. He therefore shifted Sharon from the Ministry of Agriculture to the Defence Ministry — a great sacrifice on his part, for it is well known that Begin had fallen in love with the ministry and made himself at home there. However, he clearly believed that the achievement of his aim was worth the sacrifice. From the Prime Minister's point of view, the move was certainly the correct one: Sharon wanted a war in Lebanon, although his reasons for launching the campaign were not entirely identical with those of Begin. The absence of complete agreement explains why the war spread beyond the goal set by Begin, which was essentially to deal a death blow to the PLO's military infrastructure. Since that aim was also part of Sharon's conception of the war, and since Begin lacked not only military experience but also strategic imagination, he could not foresee the complications which were liable to arise as a result of deviation from his original plan. Doubtless Sharon and the third in the group of decision-makers, the Chief of Staff Eitan — without whose unequivocal support the government might have refused to grant the Prime Minister the authority to start the war — did not make it clear to Begin that the agreement between them was incomplete, nor the results which were liable to follow from this.

By the very nature of the alliance between Begin and Sharon, the Prime Minister took it upon himself to provide political cover for the planned war, in Israel, within the ruling coalition, and internationally as well. The Defence Minister was free to develop the operational plan, by turns concealing and revealing the expected moves demanded by his conception. However, his general approach and *modus operandi* were well-known even before he began speaking freely about a military action; they were described in an article which the present writer published in *Haaretz* on 28 August 1981, a few days after Sharon's appointment as Minister of Defence, entitled 'Tigers Don't Eat Grass'.

This article linked Sharon's efforts to establish Israeli control over Judea, Samaria, and the Gaza Strip with his aim of dealing a crushing blow to the PLO by driving its fighters away from the northern borders of the state. That is 'is consistent with the American aim of driving the Soviets out of the region'. The means would be the IDF, 'to be used in order to clean out the area'. In other words, no more raids from the air and the sea, or incursions on land, but a massive campaign of ground forces for the purpose of crushing and eliminating the enemy.

Incidentally, it is worth giving another quotation from the article because of the light it sheds on subsequent events: 'It seems that Mr Sharon will be surprised . . . by the inconsistency of his inter-locutors (the Americans)'. This inconsistency was revealed when the United States refrained from declaring its support for Israel in response to the Soviet warning against continued attacks on the Syrian army at the end of the first week of Operation Peace for the Galilee, during the siege of Beirut, and also after the IDF entered the Lebanese capital.

Two conclusions emerge from the article: in 1981 Sharon's plan of the military operation had not yet been fully formulated to include the removal of the Syrian army from Lebanon; further, at this time there was no US plan for what should be done in Lebanon. However, perhaps influenced by Major-General Eitan, the removal of the Syrians from Lebanon by dealing a stiff blow to their forces there subsequently became an integral part of Sharon's plans, equal in importance to the original goal, the destruction of the PLO command and the physical removal of its leaders. Moreover, the US Government was also obliged to take notice of the impending war on Israel's northern border, to no small degree because of the pressure of the Israeli Defence Minister, who gave lectures on his operational plans in Lebanon, illustrating them with a map spread out for the convenience of his listeners; among others he spoke to both the senior staff of the American Embassy in Israel and Administration officials in Washington. In any case, Begin, Foreign Minister Shamir, and Sharon lost very few opportunities of explaining to the Americans that their intention of settling accounts with the PLO in Lebanon was serious; and finally the United States got the message. As to the operational agreement between Israel and the Reagan Administration, there are differences of opinion. Some people point to the explicit US reservations about Israeli military operations in Lebanon, which were given wide publicity by the use of deliberate leaks from closed meetings; others hold that Israel, that is, the Prime Minister and the Defence Minister, had sound reasons to believe that the Lebanese operation enjoyed support and even sympathy among the American leaders, especially the influential Secretary of State, Alexander Haig.

Before the curtain rose on the Lebanese drama, this is how the scenario appeared to the principal players. Menachem Begin saw very clearly the expulsion of the PLO from the vicinity of the border with Israel, and in more hazy outline, the destruction of its military and political infrastructure. Ariel Sharon saw the IDF's conquest of Beirut, assisted by those whom he viewed as the fighters of the Maronite militias; at the same time, he clearly envisaged the rout of the Syrian army and its being driven out of Lebanon. At the same time the US Administration, that is, those of its representatives who were involved in the matter, projected a picture of Lebanon ruled by a pro-Western government, after the PLO, a Soviet ally, had suffered a military defeat and lost its status in south Lebanon. As later emerged from a remark made by Secretary of State Haig in a conversation with the Israeli ambassador in Washington, the US Administration was pleased — in keeping with the logic of the overall approach of the United States applied to the conflict in the north-eastern corner of the Mediterranean — with the blow which Israel dealt to the Syrians, the protégés of the Soviet Union. ('You are doing great and important work for everybody in Lebanon', Haig is reported to have said.) The differences in the scenarios were ultimately to make the package fall apart. The Americans, as is their wont, wanted an independent Lebanon liberated from the PLO (and the Syrians), but they did not agree to the brutal methods, such as those adopted by the IDF during the siege of Beirut, however necessary they might have been to achieve their goals. Similarly the campaign against Syria, which Sharon regarded as essential and which he conducted more often than not by misleading his colleagues and the Prime Minister (whose understanding of the operational logic of military moves was minimal), strained to the breaking point the bonds of the alliance that had been forged between the Minister of Defence and Menachem Begin.

The Failure of the War

The opening moves of the war vindicated the high hopes of its initiators: the PLO was routed and ejected from southern Lebanon, the air force smashed the Syrian air force and knocked out the anti-aircraft missiles deployed in the Beka Valley, thereby exorcising the fears left over from the Yom Kippur War. The number of casualties, although higher than predicted, was still within tolerable limits when compared to the results. Not surprisingly, these successes were followed by self-congratulatory declarations by the Prime Minister and the Minister of Defence. However, after a fortnight the campaign stalled: the IDF found it difficult to cope with the problems inherent in conquering a major city held by guerrilla fighters who knew how to exploit the cover of its buildings and ruins; the number of casualties began to slip out of control; in the international arena Israel was overwhelmed by a well orchestrated campaign of hatred of an intensity unknown since the dark days of the UN resolution identifying Zionism with racism. The Americans quickly abandoned the sinking ship and initiated contacts with the PLO and Jordan, from which the Reagan Plan emerged later on; in Israel, public opinion became solid against the war, for after August 1982 it achieved nothing but further casualties. There is reason to believe that even if the Kahan Commission had not come up with its findings regarding the responsibility for the massacres in Sabra and Shatila, Sharon would probably have been forced to face public judgement.

Menachem Begin, who apparently sincerely believed that the campaign in Lebanon would proceed in line with his conception of it, removing the PLO from its territorial bases with the precision of a surgeon's scalpel, in other words, without involving Israel in a costly war or causing a rift with the United States, did not find it difficult, when the Kahan Commission pointed an accusing finger at the Defence Minister, to cut his links with Sharon. However, justice is not always done or seen to be done; thus Begin was applauded at the time for getting rid of Sharon, although he was actually evading his own responsibility as the initiator of a war that was ending badly.

In retrospect, the failure of the war, the price of which was greater than the benefits it brought, is attributable to two fundamental flaws: the Israeli public was not morally prepared for it — which is not surprising, considering that its goals were not agreed upon even between the Prime Minister and the Minister of Defence; and there was no full discussion with the United States, whose assistance was vital in the international arena, in which only elements hostile to Israel were then active. But while Begin was not immediately called to account for his misjudgments, for the like of which Golda Meir was removed from office, they continued to dog him and later brought about his disappearance from the national stage.

On 20 August 1982, the last month of his Lebanese euphoria, preceding the months of remorse and depression which overcame him after he learned of the Phalangist massacres in the Palestinian refugee camps, Menachem Begin gave a lecture at the National Defence College, in which he responded to the arguments against the war with the PLO which he had unleashed in Lebanon, thus anticipating the harsh criticism which was later to be directed against him. Begin's thesis is summed up in the conclusion to the lecture:

> It follows, both on the basis of international relations and as a result of our own national experience, that we are not obligated to make war only when there is no other alternative. . . . Such a war might end in disaster, if not holocaust, for any country, and cause dreadful casualties. . . . It is incumbent upon a free nation . . . concerned for its security, to create the conditions such that its wars, if it must fight them, *will not be fought in the absence of an alternative.*

Begin's final emphasis was misplaced, however: his opponents and critics disagreed with the necessity of the war in Lebanon, not with the principle that when vital interests are at stake, and when the enemy is about to start a war, it is permissible, even imperative, to launch a pre-emptive strike. The question of whether or not to go to war in these circumstances is academic: politicians and their military advisers usually agree that in such circumstances — and this is what characterises them — the two previously mentioned conditions have been met. The message that the Prime Minister sought to insinuate into the minds of his listeners was something entirely different: an application of von Clausewitz's generalisation that war is the continuation of politics by other means, to the Arab-Israeli conflict. Or, in plain English: 'If I have an obnoxious enemy who is weaker than myself but unwilling to yield, I may, even though he does not endanger my existence, start a war against him and prosecute it with every means at my disposal'. In fact, to Begin's mind, the war in Lebanon was modelled on that formula. The historical example with which the Prime Minister sought to illustrate the need for a pre-emptive attack was the salami method of conquest used by Hitler in Central Europe before the Second World War. If the French and British had made a pre-emptive move when the German dictator announced the cancellation of the Versailles treaty, they might have successfully nipped his plans in the bud. However, this illustration is absurd, for there was no comparison between the respective strengths of the IDF and the PLO and those of Britain and France, on the one hand, and that which Hitler already possessed in 1936. In fact the Prime Minister's reasoning takes us back much further than the generalisations distilled by the philosophers of war from historical experience. In a nutshell, what he said was that the strong devour the weak. The lecture was pure Darwin for beginners.

The Future of Likud

It seems that as disappointment with the war in Lebanon became increasingly evident — disappointment may be defined as the perception of the disproportion between the gains from the war and the price paid in terms of lives and money — the national agenda initially formulated after the Six Day War was nearing the end of its lifespan. Consequently the Likud, which was identified with that national agenda, had come to the point in history where Mapai had been after the elections of 1959: from then on the curve turned downwards. Two parallels might serve to illustrate the point. From 1959 on Mapai was caught up in a ferocious fight for David Ben-Gurion's political inheritance; and since early 1983 the Likud, or rather Herut, has been locked in a struggle for Menachem Begin's political legacy. The second parallel lies in the area where the crisis occurred. For Mapai it was domestic matters which were the main focus of the national agenda peculiar to the party. The crisis took the form of the collapse — despite efforts to maintain them — of its organisational structures, and later as the recession struck, of beliefs in the fundamental strength of the economy. With the Likud the crisis was centred on foreign affairs, the struggle for territory, for international status, etc. Lebanon demarcated the limits of Israeli power. It did not necessarily follow that the end of Likud rule was at hand; Mapai continued to hold the reins for another decade and a half after it had exhausted the national agenda with which it was identified. But the change in government, not one that is merely technical in character but which signals more than the mere replacement of the party in power, became more likely.

Appropriately, the Likud, or rather the Herut Movement, limits the demands it addresses to the country to the area of power and politics: the nation must mobilise for a greater Israel and its status in the world — national glory, in Jabotinskian terms. For the rest, the Likud is permiissive in character. It does not ask for personal commitment as did the Labour Movement in its years of glory; it does not demand moral superiority in the manner of Ben-Gurion, who wanted Israel to be a light unto the nations; and even more conspicuous by its absence in the Likud's political creed is the command to strive for economic independence. Menachem Begin coined the slogan, 'To do well by the people'. The actual formulation of the concept, though more obscure, is not to ask much from the people, but to let them act according to their own lights and instincts. Theoretically this suits Likud's ideological liberalism and its next of kin, social Darwinism. However, the slogan needs to be amended to state that the poor must be attended to not only for the sake of humanity, but also because of their importance as voters.

Connoisseurs of social paradox could do worse than take a look at Likud, especially its main component, Herut. Zeev Jabotinsky, the founding father and spiritual mentor of Herut, was the son of a wealthy Jewish bourgeois family in Czarist Russia. He himself was a liberal intellectual, a true *fin de siècle* European, victim of the Nietzschean fashion then current among intellectuals (see, for example, his definition of the national ideal in the anthem, of the movement he formed, 'genial and generous and cruel', as well as his enthusiasm for Italian fascism, especially for Gabriele D'Annunzio). However, from the political school founded, nurtured, and guided spiritually by Jabotinsky, there arose a party which many people call populist, but which might be more accurately termed plebeian: its members and functionaries are run of the mill, not exactly the elite of the citizenry, and its leaders, with very few exceptions, are second-raters, not particularly well educated or endowed with vision. The style of public debate typical of Herut is well suited to its social composition: it addresses emotions and instincts, and its devotion to the principle of a leader, raised above the multitude, gave the State of Israel the kind of feebly authoritarian leadership which has become its trademark.

We have so far discussed three principal decisions taken by Menachem Begin after taking power in 1977: the peace treaty with Egypt, the settlement policy and the war in Lebanon. The fourth decision had its roots in his permissive social outlook. It was implemented in two stages. First, Yigael Horowitz, the Finance Minister who advocated fiscal severity, was dismissed in late 1980.

Yoram Aridor was then appointed in his place and enjoined to execute an economic policy that would help the Likud in the rapidly approaching election campaign. In the second stage, after winning the 1981 elections, it was decided to continue this permissive policy. We shall discuss the technical aspects of Aridor's policy in the following chapter. Suffice it to say here that his policies led to a profound crisis in the summer of 1983, which came to a head simultaneously with the other, the political and security crisis of Begin's second term, following the war in Lebanon.

Once the votes in the 1981 elections were counted, and the seats apportioned to the party lists, interpretations began to emerge, including an evaluation of what the election results meant for the longer term. One conclusion, perhaps the most interesting in a mixed lot, was that the Likud had become the long-term majority party. Those who were of this opinion based their conclusion on the fact that in absolute terms the Likud had continued to grow at a fast rate, whereas its Labour rival, which had apparently grown at an even faster rate, was merely recovering the voters it had lost to the Democratic Movement for Change in the previous elections.

However, this conclusion invites both further comment and some qualification. After the 1977 elections, commentators, both publicists and academics, differed as to the source of the votes that had been attracted to the DMC, which had only come into existence a year before. It received 200,000 votes, nearly 12 per cent of the valid ballots, and it was represented by fifteen Knesset members. Some claimed that most of the DMC voters came from Labour's pool of voters, and thus Labour was the party most damaged by the new party. Other analysts, such as Naham Urieli and Amnon Barzilai, in their book *The Rise and Fall of the DMC*,[6] believed that if the DMC had not existed, disappointed Labour voters would have voted for the Likud. Thus both the major parties were harmed by the DMC, although Urieli and Barzilai refrain from estimating the relative extent of the damage. The results of the 1981 elections, however, ought to have put an end to that particular dispute. Apart from 30,000 voters who voted for the heir of the DMC, a splinter party called Shinui (Change), most of the votes which had gone to the DMC returned to Labour, the number of whose voters grew from 430,000 to 708,000 in 1981. A similar picture emerges from a comparison of the number of votes given to Labour in 1977 and in 1973: they fell from 621,000 in 1973 to 430,000 in 1977, the difference being about he number of votes received by the DMC.

Let us now examine the proposition that the Likud has become the party of the future as a result of its continued dynamic growth. The statistics provide only partial support for this assumption, as indicated by Table 4.1.

Some commentators, in comparing the figures for 1977 and 1981, did not include Shlomtsion voters, although that party joined the Likud after the elections to the ninth Knesset. If that factor is neglected, it could be argued that Likud had grown by 23 per cent between the eighth and ninth Knesset elections and again between the ninth and tenth Knessets. In fact, the growth was only 16 per cent when adjusted for Shlomtsion, and if the overall increase in the number of voters is also deducted, the percentage increase declines from 11.5 to 5 per cent. The picture thus emerging is therefore not one of continued rapid growth but rather of a curve which has passed its peak.

If this conclusion is correct, it contradicts another hypothesis based on empirical experience as follows: (i) Oriental Jews prefer the Likud; (ii) the proportion of Oriental Jews within the electorate is rising; (iii) therefore henceforth the proportion of the Likud in the electorate must increase. This hypothesis is not, however, supported by the results of the elections to the ninth and tenth Knessets. There is no proof, that the ethnic factor in the voters' choice between the Likud and Labour will remain stable over the long term. Two researchers, Asher Arian and Michal Shamir,[7] basing their work on opinion polls taken before and after Knesset

Table 4.1 Distribution of Knesset votes, 1973, 1977, 1981

	1973	1977	1981
Number of Voters (millions)	1.6	1.8	2.0
Likud Voters (without Sharon's Shlomtsion Party)(000s)	473	584	——
Likud Voters (including Shlomtsion) (000s)	——	——	718
% Increase for Likud (without Shlomtsion)		23	——
% Increase for Likud (including Shlomtsion)		——	16
% Increase for Likud (including Shlomtsion in 1981, but minus the increase attributable to the general increase in the number of voters)		11.5	5

elections since the 1960s, have shown that one can isolate two elements which are statistically correlated with ethnicity, and which affect voting in a discernible manner: traditionalism and hawkishness. It appears that Oriental Jews tend to be more traditional and hawkish. This has also been the Likud image in the past and will continue to be so in the future. However, it has not been shown that traditionalism is a collective characteristic enduring over time; and as for hawkishness, it is not yet sufficiently clear how that feature will survive the shocks of the war in Lebanon.

In the following chapter we shall discuss the economic and social aspects of the Likud Government, but it should be mentioned here that, although Mapai laid the foundations of the welfare state, the Likud gave particular prominence to the welfare character of its policies. The Labour Party, faithful to its ideological sources, attributed special value to work and logically demanded a decent reward for participation in the process of production. The Likud's basic approach is different: less attention must be paid to an economic function such as work, more to the status of the citizen in society, such as being old, or a member of a large family or subject to a physical handicap, and so on. The contest between these two approaches, of which the Likud's is more fashionable, is still being waged, not only in Israel but throughout the West; its outcome could be highly influential in determining the future of the Likud as a long-term ruling party.

The Begin Era

It is said that the Likud-Herut Movement has no history, only the biography of its leader, Menachem Begin. Certainly there can be no question about his dominance as founder and anchor of stability during twenty-nine long years marred by repeated electoral defeats, and as final arbiter whose views and management of current policy were unchallenged. It is too soon to say whether he was one of the political greats, as his admirers believe, or merely a successful demagogue as his rivals say. What is clear is that Menachem Begin made his mark on the history of Israel and of the region and strengthened the morale of a people confused and depressed in the aftermath of the Yom Kippur War, but he also exposed them to the danger of disaster.

An outstanding politician has many facets. Two characteristics of

Begin's kind of statesmanship should be emphasised, in that they were peculiar to him: his method for raising the country's morale, and his use of the memory of the Holocaust as a source of national atonement. In describing these traits, one has to indulge in speculation as to his motives. Admittedly, it is impossible to enter the heart and soul of another man; nevertheless, hypotheses on the subject, if they are not clearly contradicted by facts, must be permissible. Without a modicum of speculation, the study of history in all its variety becomes mere chronology.

We have already said that the Yom Kippur War and its aftermath in Israel, in the diaspora, and in the non-Jewish world, left the Israeli public confused and sunk in a sea of depression, from which the Labour Party and its government, which had long since turned into mere administrators with no vision, could not lift it. Menachem Begin took power, presumably in the firm belief that Providence had charged him with freeing the people from the nightmare of failure. In the world of Darwinian ideas in which Begin lives, standing upright implies forcing one's fellow man to bend; one pushes around anyone who is standing still and one challenges those who are or pretend to be sufficiently big and strong to lay down the law to those around them, but whose determination, in fact, is weaker than it appears. This was, in fact, the blue-print guiding the Prime Minister's actions even during his first term of office, as witness his appointment of Ariel Sharon as the minister in effective control of the occupied territories, on the one hand, and his clear signalling of the limits of Israel's willingness to withdraw, on the other.

He expressed these views in his talks with President Carter during his first visit to Washington in the summer of 1977. Even then one could see the first signs of the methods he was about to use in order to stiffen Israel's resolve. For some time diplomatic circumstances forced him to delay the process, but after signing the peace treaty with President Sadat and getting rid of two troublesome ministers, Dayan and Weitzmann, he could once again do as he pleased: suppress Arab irridentism in Palestine, not infrequently by excessive force; escalate the battle against the PLO and its allies in Lebanon; destroy the nuclear reactor in Iraq (incidentally, knowledgable people have more than once expressed reservations regarding the necessity of that action for Israel's security); say 'No' repeatedly to the United States; make public personal attacks on prominent foreign statesmen; and as the *pièce de résistance*, verbally whiplash the US ambassador in a conversation bearing all the characteristics of Begin, the demagogue — all these were stations along the way. The decision to go to war in Lebanon cannot be fully understood if one ignores Begin's wish to stiffen the nation's backbone by smashing the weak and challenging the strong. Perhaps even his arrogant self-praise, the identifying mark of the successful Begin, was merely a slight exaggeration for the sake of helping along the psychotherapeutic process which he had begun in order to shake the country out of its depression.

In retrospect, one can say that the confusion and depression of Yom Kippur no longer plague the country. However, this achievement, perhaps a result of Begin's therapy, and perhaps, at least partially, the result of the passage of time, has exacted a rather high price, whether in terms of relations between Jews and Arabs, or in terms of the animosity of foreign politicians and countries whom the Prime Minister engaged in verbal battles or whose interests he actually damaged, and, above all, in terms of the damage to national unity. Indeed, Menachem Begin divided the country far more than any of his predecessors.

Begin was not the first to be called the King of the Jews. There was another whom the people, not a few of them mockingly, called the King of the Jews. He too was what one calls these days a social demagogue, and of him it was also said that he undermined the colonial authority then ruling the country. The man in question, Jesus of Nazareth, roamed the country armed with a few simple messages, the principal one, or at least the one most readily absorbed, being his declaration that, of his own free will and in agreement with the Divinity, he had taken original sin upon himself. The concept of sin and the sense of guilt are Jewish inventions, and so it is only natural that tidings of personal atonement following the transfer of sin to the saviour, Jesus, spread rapidly among the Jews and that the bearer of this message became increasingly popular. Today it would come as no surprise to learn that there was a positive correlation between the low intelligence quotients, the poor education, and the poverty of his followers and their degree of belief in his message.

Menachem Begin bore a different message, better suited to the circumstances, the times, and his purposes. However, what was common to him and the other King of the Jews, was that they both offered atonement to their followers, not only for the sins of the past, but for eternity. Begin did this by means of the Holocaust, which exterminated one out of every three of the sons and daughters of the Jewish people, not only wiping mortal men off the face of the earth, but also destroying a civilisation and way of life which will never be seen again. It should be recalled that Begin, unlike his political rivals on the Zionist left, valued and cherished that civilisation and way of life. According to his message, since the terrors of the Holocaust have been visited upon the Jewish people, it can sin no more. In the great account book on high in which the deeds of men and nations are registered, with credit entries balanced by debits, there is in the Jewish account no longer any debit column. This in brief, was Begin's quasi-religious message; and since the Jewish people, even in its secularity, is a nation of faith, as can be seen from its ceaseless preoccupation with morality and justice (for which there is no guarantee or sanction other than the divine one), Begin's message found eager listeners, their attention proportionate to the weight attached to faith, rather than critical intelligence, in their mental make-up.

Israel is a nation whose recent past has redeemed it from sin: it would be difficult to find a message that speaks more suggestively to the depths of the people's innermost being, and this serves to explain the quasi-religious sentiments which Menachem Begin aroused in many parts of the community. Did the Prime Minister deliberately exploit their feelings and the associations he aroused by recalling the Holocaust over and over again, or did he do so unconsciously, the way politicians do in constantly referring to topics which concern them, whether they are relevant or not? This question must be answered by social psychologists. Suffice it to point out here that Begin proclaimed redemption; there is no better explanation of why a politician, whose failures had made him a laughing stock in the eyes of Israel's social and political elite, became a leader respected by a much larger number of his fellow countrymen than the rather limited nucleus of Herut loyalists. He was not an efficient party boss, nor yet a great statesman, and certainly not a military leader; even as a demagogue and a prophet of frustration and hatred, there have been others more venomous. But he preached the message of a certain kind of redemption. The fact that he divided the country is not surprising; preachers of redemption have always been divisive.

Notes

1. Zeev Jabotinsky (1880–1940), a Zionist leader, founder of the Revisionist Zionist Alliance, the forerunner of Herut.

2. Yaakov Shavit, *From Majority to State* (Hebrew) (Yariv-Hadar, Tel Aviv, 1978).

3. The Society for the Land of Israel was established after the Six Day War to promote the idea that the land west of the Jordan is the historical patrimony of the Jewish people and should be subject to Israeli sovereignty.

4. Tsvi Raanan, *Gush Emunim* (Hebrew) (Sifriat Hapoalim, Tel Aviv, 1980).

5. A heretical movement that swept through world Jewry during the seventeenth century, following the appearance of the false messiah Sabbatai Sevi.

6. Nahman Urieli and Amnon Barzilai, *The Rise and Fall of the DMC* (Hebrew) (Reshafim, Tel Aviv, 1982).

7. Asher Arian and Michal Shamir, 'The Ethnic Vote in Israel's 1981 Elections' *Electoral Studies*, 1, 1982, pp. 315–31.

5 TRANSFORMATIONS

The Jewish settlement (the *Yishuv*) in Palestine during the period of the Mandate can deservedly be called a state in the making. With one exception: it did not concern itself with economic absorption, apart from the absorption of agricultural settlers. These were acknowledged to be worthy of public support, in that they were carrying out a national mission: the settlement of barren and remote places in the country, sometimes cut off from the centres of the Jewish population. Their status was similar to that of IDF soldiers sent on a mission.

This explains the character of agricultural settlement, which was never intended to become fully profitable, in terms either of the resources made available to it by the responsible institutions or the concepts of the time. The socialist views of the settlers and their organisations combined with their lack of independent capital and the national imperatives to which land settlement, according to the outlook of the leaders of the Zionist movement, was meant to respond. Candidates for agricultural settlement were supported by the institutions of the *Yishuv* and of the Zionist movement: they were trained abroad, brought to the country, consolidated as a group, and sent to settle in places chosen for them, using the resources put at their disposal. While the arrival of other kinds of immigrants also gladdened the hearts of the Jewish inhabitants of Palestine and they too were wanted and lobbied for by the Zionist movement, which sought to bring in as many Jews as possible, those who came on their own had to support themselves. Upon their arrival in the cities or towns, they had to stand in queues at the employment bureaus as did the veterans. If they had funds of their own, they opened stores, workshops, or factories — all on their own initiative and at their own risk.

This outlook remained in force during the early years of the state as well. Agriculture was a planned branch of the economy, and those who joined it, whether veteran settlers or new immigrants, went through an institutionalised process of absorption. Other new members of the labour force, whether they lived in hastily erected tent cities, in towns, or in the cities, were expected to find employment in the cities or in the development projects undertaken by the government or the Jewish Agency. It can be said that during the first five or six years following the establishment of the state, the dual character of the economy was preserved: part of it, largely the agricultural sector, was planned, while the remaining sectors were governed by market conditions, i.e. business initiative, competition, supply and demand, etc. (An exception to this generalisation is, of course, the government sector, including the Jewish Agency and the municipal bureaucracies, whose share of national income grew greatly in comparison with the period of the Mandate. This could also be defined as an absorbing sector of the economy, with features placing it somewhere between planned agriculture and unplanned urban enterprise.)

Those who implemented the settler-statist national agenda guiding the actions of the national leadership at that time, wanted a large part, if not the majority, of the new members of the labour force to be absorbed in agriculture for their ideology demanded the upending of the Jewish economic pyramid. Moreover, the vital need to fill the regions left empty by the flight of the Arab inhabitants during the War of Independence also cried out for agricultural settlements. Finally, agricultural settlement suited the self-image of the Zionist movement as one which was meant not only to redeem the people from its exile but also to redeem the land from its barrenness. One might add here that, while economic absorption in agriculture was the most thorough going, it was also the most tightly controlled. Given the conditions of the mass immigration of highly diverse communities, this characteristic had to be seen as an important advantage, perhaps a decisive one, in the light of the absorption apparatus. Farming and not urban communities seemed the preferable melting pot. Nevertheless, the basic facts of the economy prevented the 'productivisation' of the majority of the immigrants by way of agriculture. During the Mandate an endless dispute was waged between the Jewish community and the mandatory authorities, who argued against uncontrolled immigration, claiming that the absorptive capacity of Palestine was limited, given the limited availability of fertile soil, water, etc. The economists of the Zionist movement, men such as Robert Nathan, Oscar Gass, and Daniel Kramer in their book, *Palestine, Problem and Promise*,[1] argued against this view, claiming 'The reserves of land, water, and other natural resources are not the basic factors determining the extent of economic development that can be achieved in the coming decade'. They did concede that 'Agriculture will receive a less important permanent status in the structure of Jewish employment than it enjoyed during the thirties'. What these economists foresaw in 1946, when their book was published, was what the government actually encountered after the establishment of the state: the form of productivisation, which the leadership considered the most satisfactory for masses of immigrants, proved to be of limited potential, just as Nathan and his colleagues had foreseen. Between 1948 and 1954 the supply of Jewish manpower grew by about 300,000. Agriculture absorbed about 20,000 employees, less than 7 per cent of those who joined the potential work force. The main reason for this disappointing performance was the relative shortage of resources available to the absorbers: the scarce primary physical resource was water — but Jewish agriculture was based on irrigation. The Zionist movement's economists estimated that available water resources were some 2.84 million cubic metres, an estimate which proved unduly optimistic (in 1983 Israel used approximately 1.7 million cubic metres of water, including quantities supplied by the National Water Carrier).

As mentioned previously, the principal issue that forced itself upon the leaders of the state immediately after its establishment, and one upon which they concentrated to the exclusion of all others, was the absorption of the masses of immigrants pouring into the country. The government was forced to channel resources, which it did not actually have, to provide the primary needs of the immigrants and put a roof over their heads, even if only a very rudimentary one. Both Zionist ideology and common sense told the political and administrative elites that it was insufficient to supply what was needed for mere subsistence and nothing more. Agriculture, the most highly developed and preferred absorptive branch, could only support a limited number of immigrants: and its limitations grew increasingly apparent with the passage of time. By 1954–5 the absorptive capacity of agriculture had reached its limits. In the meantime the cities and towns had filled with immigrants, who made a living of sorts in industry, construction, and the services, areas of activity that did not receive planned government funding, apart from the civil service and its branches and the make-work projects for the unemployed. However, it was evident that these branches of the economy could no longer support the burden of economic absorption on their own. They could not expand and develop, at least not according to the rules then applying in Israeli society.

Countries which go through a process of mass immigration generally solve the problems of absorption by lowering real income: the marginal immigrant prepared to work for the minimum necessary for his sustenance determines the level of wages. According to economic theory, in such situations entrepreneurs are found, or ought to be found, who somehow raise the capital necessary to transform the immigrants from people dependent upon public support to self-supporting workers. Moreover, the low real wages go hand in hand with a currency undervalued in terms of purchasing power parity, which in turn helps to attract capital to the country absorbing the immigrants and to encourage exports from it as well. However, Israel took the opposite path. The political elites derived support from the labour movement with a strong trade-unionist tradition; anyone wishing to absorb immigration against that background had to guarantee real wages and attract capital even though investment might not have been attractive from a business point of view. Thus Israel had to support a chronic import surplus needed to provide a decent standard of living for an under-productive society, as well as an over-valued currency. The decisive achievement of the Mapai regime, without which it is doubtful whether it would have been possible almost to double the original population within the first three or four years of the state, was the importation of foreign capital on an unprecedented scale compared with the size of the Israeli economy. Of necessity, this capital was not imported on a commercial basis. The mechanisms invented and activated by Mapai, from the effective raising of contributions in the prosperous Jewish communities abroad to the issuing of interest-bearing bonds denominated in dollars and negotiating international transfer payments (German reparations and loans from the United States), were unique. The Likud Governments, although no less thirsty for funds, never displayed talents like those of the first Israeli governments or showed the same creativity and practical organisa-tional ability in obtaining economic assistance to subsidise absorption and development.

Critics of the economic rules of the game instituted by the Mapai regime and of the 'shnorr' (Yiddish for begging) as an undignified way of providing for the needs of the economy — the more so as they encouraged dependence — were correct in pointing out the distortions they caused. It is true that those who live on charity become accustomed to consuming more than they produce either by physical or intellectual work. The result is parasitism and dependence on those who hand out the money and demand nothing in return. However, the Mapai leaders could argue against their critics that the process of productivisation which they launched during the first years after the establishment of the state, created a healthy and functioning society, the very opposite of a consciously and openly parasitic way of life. As for dependence on donors, it is doubtful whether a country the size of Israel existing in an environment noteworthy for its extreme hostility, could have been any freer in its decisions had it not received foreign aid. More than anything else, it is doubtful whether the veteran settlers would have agreed to the mass absorption of immigrants had they known it would necessitate a steep and prolonged decline in the standard of living to which they had become used (and which was not, in any case, particularly high). In retrospect it can be said that the actions taken by the political and administrative elites during the first years of the state were sensible in terms of that period.

The key words in the foregoing sentence are 'that period'. Twenty to thirty years later, the economic habits which originated in the 1950s and perhaps even earlier, diverted public attention from the first principle of accounting, which is that the books must balance — perhaps not every year, but at least they must average out over the years. It became customary to think that if one came to the end of one's tether, the government would rush to the rescue, since the government had an unlimited bank account, which Uncle Sam or some other provider would replenish whenever necessary. Thus the granting of favours to one sort of citizen or another was seen to depend only on the good will of legislators or administrators, not on objective constraints limiting what could actually be given away. This approach was accompanied by a policy of over-valuing the Israeli Pound, and afterwards the Sheqel. As a result, exporting became more difficult and, conversely, imports were encouraged. Thus a pattern of over-consumption was created, without taking into account the ultimate results, either in the domestic economy or in its effect on the balance of payments. The Likud governments did very little to change these patterns, even though the parties of which they were composed had been its most vocal critics whilst in opposition. In the mid-1960s, a momentous period during which certain decisions which shaped an entire generation were taken, the time had been ripe for a fundamental change in the country's economic ways, away from the political and economic circumstances created during the first decade. An effort could have been made to normalise the average Israeli's attitude towards the basic economic categories of 'have' and 'have not'. However, that change was never made, and the results are clear for all to see.

Industrialisation Policy

By the end of the 1950s it had become abundantly clear that the disappointing rate of absorption in agriculture was a permanent phenomenon, both because of the high cost of creating an agricultural production unit, and because of the scarcity of available physical resources, especially water. At the same time the government's efforts to raise capital began to bear fruit: contributions, raised in the diaspora, dollar bonds, reparations — all these gave the Treasury extensive financial resources. Fortunately it was decided not to waste them on current expenditures. There was no shortage of potential workers; on the contrary, there was an embarrassing abundance. In what economic sector should they be absorbed so as to turn them into productive workers? The question carried its own answer; once agriculture was removed from the list as the absorber of the masses, only industry was left. Since the Second World War it had employed about a quarter of the Jewish labour force. The government therefore decided to put their development money into industry, and as a sign of the firmness of that decision they placed the matter in the hands of one of their own people: Pinhas Sapir, a man who had earned a reputation as an achiever.

This decision was not an easy or self-evident one. Industry had previously enjoyed encouragement neither from the Jewish Agency nor from the State of Israel. Certainly it did not obey the instructions of the Party. The prominent industrialists belonged to the bourgeois camp, the traditional rival of the Palestine Workers' Party. While there were several industrial firms belonging to the Histadrut, organised within the administrative framework of Koor (the manufacturing concern), Solel Boneh (the construction company) and Hamashbir Hamerkazi (the wholesale organisation), it was clear to Sapir and those he represented that anyone devoting himself to the task of industrial development must accept the additional risk entailed in acting in an unknown and potentially unfriendly arena. There was a further risk because as soon as the decision was made to give government encouragement to industrialisation, the question arose of where to invest the money originating in the government budget.

In very general terms, this question did not arise in agriculture. Or, more precisely, it had arisen and been answered years before: according to standard procedures, public monies were invested in the establishment of additional mixed agricultural units, based on a few acres of irrigated fields whose produce was mainly intended for the local market. The co-operative agricultural settlements hardly grew any produce for export: their share in citrus production began to increase only after the local market for vegetables had been saturated.

What direction, then, should be given to the effort at industrialisation? The government had no ready answer, and there was no one in Israel who could advise or direct it. However, there was the example provided by the branch in which rich experience in public funding had been accumulated: agriculture. The leadership, the Minister of Finance, Levi Eshkol, and the recently appointed Minister of Trade and Industry, Pinhas Sapir, set out to plan on the agricultural model. The course of action was determined by the outlines of a given local market, on the one hand, and given productive factors on the other. Industry in Palestine had taken great strides during the Second World War: the lack of transport facilities had provided effective protection against foreign competition; the lack of foreign exchange after the establishment of the state also acted as a defensive wall protecting local production. Now this wall had only to be reinforced by customs duties and home-grown administrative procedures to create a well protected local market.

Nevertheless the question remained of the direction industrialisation was to take, that is, the steps to be taken after sufficient attention had been given to supplying the local market. It should be added that during the mid-1950s the local market was unsophisticated and undemanding, very different from that of the 1980s as far as variety and quality were concerned. In other countries which have undergone the process of industrialisation, entrepreneurs from the private sector set the direction of future growth, even in Third World countries like Taiwan, with a similar history of rapid industrialisation. However in Israel, where the rules of the game were unique, it was difficult for the private sector to guide industrial development to the extent necessary to supply permanent employment for a rapidly growing population as well as for the currently unemployed and underemployed. Previous means of absorption had not been sufficient to engage them in the productive process, nor did the Mapai economic regime place sufficient trust in businessmen, who were the traditional supporters of rival parties, to entrust them with considerable economic resources to be invested as they saw fit. Here then the reluctance of the donors met the incapacity of the potential recipients. This combination of circumstances led to industrialisation subsidised and directed by the government, and planned according to the example of agriculture: in other words supply, not demand, was to provide the potential for development.

In schematic fashion one can describe the planning process as follows. In a given year so many job-seekers reach the labour market, distributed in such and such proportions among the different regions of the country. Industry needs electricity, raw materials, etc. Of these the government was able to supply a certain quantity. The missing factor was someone to organise production, a person or a body with some experience and knowledge in the establishment and running of firms of a certain size — in economic parlance, an entrepreneur. At this stage the search for entrepreneurs became a prime task, and it was placed in the hands of the minister for industrialisation, Pinhas Sapir. He provided either all or most of the necessary capital, thus making the tame entrepreneur properly dependent upon the government. Investment proposals were prepared jointly by Sapir and his staff and assessed, among other things, according to formulas which set the relationship between the capital invested, employment, and profit, and by the captive entrepreneur who might or might not have contributed his own ideas to the process, but who claimed to be experienced and to possess some executive ability. From the point of view of the entrepreneur, the investment entailed no actual risk: the capital was not his in any case. He was justified in supposing that whoever had supplied him with the money, would also make sure that his investment remained profitable. In this way a bond of mutual reliance was forged between the government, which supplied the food, and those who fed at its table, the class of entrepreneurs. At the same time, the real purpose was also served: a large number of plants were established in branches of production considered to be labour-intensive; in other words, they provided a relatively large amount of employment for every pound invested in equipment, buildings, etc.

As in agricultural development, which was limited by a shortage of water, limitations in the above pattern of industrialisation soon came to light: limits in the skill and industrial experience of all the participants. The entrepreneurs' industrial experience was most often limited to theoretical knowledge or practical training in one of the traditional branches of manufacturing, such as food processing, building materials, or textiles. The government bureaucracy was a further limiting factor. Industrial plant was therefore set up on a large scale, providing employment but generally lacking the ability to compete internationally, a feature which had not been emphasised from the start among the criteria for its establishment. However, this sort of industrialisation, as long as it enjoyed protection from external competition through customs barriers and administrative restrictions (such as import licencing) which were difficult to penetrate, and as long as it did not begin to produce substantial surpluses which could not be sold locally, satisfied the chief requirement of its initiators: employment for all. The five years between 1955 and 1960 represented the height of Pinhas Sapir's career: he industrialised the country; in other words, he created jobs and sources of livelihood in industry. In so doing he resembled his colleague, Levi Eshkol, who in the first five years of the state had filled the empty expanses of the country with hundreds of Jewish settlements, into which tens of thousands of families were absorbed. It is no exaggeration to say that these two men determined the general outlines of the productive map of Israel during the first decade of its existence.·

The availability of extensive financial resources deriving from unilateral transfers from abroad, raised on the initiative of the heads of the Israeli Government, served, as if by the way to point up the real bottleneck in the industrialisation process: the evident scarcity of entrepreneurs and administrative staff, without whom industry cannot operate. We have already described how the man in charge of industrialisation, Pinhas Sapir, mobilised entrepreneurs, both real and apparent, from every available source, placing enormous sums, in the terms of those times, at their disposal, and in effect freeing them from worry about economic survival, if only they built industrial plants all over the country and employed job-seekers productively. Even at that time a question arose, not in regard to the need to find entrepreneurs as quickly as possible and staff to assist them, but in regard to the ownership of the resources placed at their disposal. It was widely held that the government ought to establish industrial plants and retain ownership over them. The entrepreneurs netted by Pinhas Sapir brought no capital of their own. In most cases the government might have been able to hire their services for a moderate fee and retain in its own hands the ownership of the assets. A solution of this kind was actually tried: public resources were distributed liberally to the economic enterprises owned by the Histadrut. At that time very few people distinguished between the Histadrut and the state, and there were quite a few enterprises owned by the Histadrut that were prepared to absorb more investment capital, so long as it did not fall into the hands of entrepreneurs in the private sector.

David Kokhav, formerly the director of the research department of Bank Israel, established in 1954, and later the senior assistant of Finance Minister Levi Eshkol, has stated[2] that a decision on this matter was taken in conversations between Eshkol and Sapir although it was not preceded by a formal debate which was officially recorded. They agreed that Israeli industry should not be controlled by the government bureaucracy as the legal owners, but that private entrepreneurs should establish manufacturing facilities with government support and manage them on their own responsibility and for their own benefit. It is possible to imagine what the reasons were for that decision, although they may have come as a surprise to those who took the socialist image of the ruling party seriously. The two men, particularly Sapir, were aware of the drawbacks of management, even of economic control, placed in the hands of officials; it is likely that they feared that administrative nationalisation through official ownership of the capital invested would have deterred contributors from the capitalist West. It is also possible that they believed that men who were willing to act as entrepreneurs in their own right would not offer their services without the tempting prospect of fat capital gains. However, to this day it is still surprising that Mapai's left-wing partners in the ruling coalition never raised their voices in protest against the system of producing capitalists with government funds. Since 1955, when the regime based on co-operation between Mapai and the General Zionists fell apart, the government depended on co-operation between Mapai, Ahdut Haavoda, and Mapam, with the General Zionists moving over into opposition. There is some irony in the fact that the material foundations of Israel's present entrepreneurial economy were laid by a regime borne on the shoulders of the Labour Movement, one in which it enjoyed a decisive majority.

In three areas of industrialisation the government did not limit itself to planning and the supply of capital, but insisted on control — in electricity generation and the exploitation of natural resources, two areas in which an unusual step was taken, not apparently in keeping with the general logic of the policy of industrialisation, namely to nationalise enterprises previously privately owned — and in the area of defence production. From an organisational point of view, the production of electricity and the industrial processing of natural resources were no different from other industrial production, in other words, they were carried out by commercial corporations. Defence production, on the other hand, was mostly concentrated within the defence establishment, i.e. it figured in the budget of the government sector of the economy. Moreover, when one looks at the character of the entrepreneur in these areas of production — an important point since the entrepreneur was the bottleneck in Israel's industrialisation — one finds substantial differences among these three branches.

The exploitation and processing of natural resources is similar, from the point of view of entrepreneurship and development, to the other industries established or expanded beyond recognition under Sapir: the basis was an existing supply of raw materials, such as potash and phosphates (and later copper), an abundant labour supply, including engineers and technicians, and a market of known size for a standard product, although a large portion of the market was foreign. The entrepreneurial model taken from agriculture was, therefore, also applicable to the industries based on local natural resources: it was supply-oriented entrepreneurship. The methods of processing producing added value were standard and to a large extent have remained so to this day; the change which took place in the scale of production over the years was largely dictated by the quantity of raw materials passing through the processing machinery. This statement should be somewhat modified, for in phosphate production an attempt was later made to upgrade the product after assessing the character of demand and anticipating changes in it, especially in foreign markets. Thus an attempt was made to go beyond the production of a standard fertiliser and to manufacture more complex and sophisticated products enjoying a competitive advantage in foreign markets. Thus a different model of industrial development emerged, one which was essentially demand-oriented.

In electricity generation, the basic data determining planning have always been the estimated demand for energy within the economy in coming years, which requires sophisticated and complex calculations, particularly in view of the long lead-time in the power generation industry. However, since the electricity company operated as a monopoly, the process of electrification did not provide a model for demand-oriented entrepreneurship with wider application.

The defence industry also was, in its first version, subject to the rules of demand-oriented enterprise. However, to a greater degree even than electricity, it was required to meet a concentrated and given demand: the IDF decided, within the framework of budgetary constraints, what and how much it would buy from the defence industry, which was subject to the same authority as the armed forces. In any case, the defence industry should not be discussed in entrepreneurial terms, although within the government bureaucracy various possibilities were considered and decisions made on entrepreneurial criteria, such as cost levels and so on. In fact, within the defence industry, which was mainly included within the budgetary framework but to some extent organised in separate corporations such as Tadiran, technical and economic considerations forced management to plan production lines for long runs or to turn out special products, some of which were meant for marketing abroad. In fact, marketing became decisive with regard to certain defence industry plants, and in the course of the time many became demand-oriented enterprises.

Two broad categories of industrialisation can thus be seen to emerge, distinguished by the driving force behind them. One type is driven by the availability of existing productive factors: a labour force in any case (for the main motivation for industrialisation in Israel was connected with the need to supply productive employment for a rapidly growing population), natural resources, and entrepreneurship arising from experience in traditional branches of production. In this category of industrialisation, which was typical of Sapir's period as Minister of Commerce and Industry, the market is regarded as given, and the entrepreneur is called upon, broadly speaking, to concentrate his efforts on organising production. This model of industrial development was quite similar to the standard model in agriculture, and to a certain degree simply required its transplantation, with some changes necessitated by the character of the product, from the one field to the other. It should be emphasised that to the degree that industrial facilities created on the supply-oriented model were intended to export anything, the planners only envisaged the export of surpluses: the basic price was set on the assumption of a protected local market — or an export market controlled by international cartels — and the potential size of this market was viewed as given, not as a specific problem whose solution would influence the profitability of production. At this time the second kind of industrialisation was beyond the scope of the government planners.

Entrepreneurship in productive plants in the second category does not begin with an inventory of available productive factors under the entrepreneur's control. It starts at the other end of the process, where there is a finished product which must be marketed. One might go even further and say that this kind of entrepreneurship begins with an abstract market survey, one which seeks to find out what is lacking; and only after a shortage is located in the market — either a natural one or one that can be created, by advertising, for example — does the entrepreneur reach the stage at which the other industrial process begins, i.e. the location and organisation of productive factors in order to satisfy the demand.

In reality, of course, the division between these two forms of industrial entrepreneurship, supply-oriented versus demand-oriented, is never as sharp as this. However, the distinction is both theoretically valid and of practical significance, especially in the Israeli economy which is not blessed with an abundance of natural resources. To limit industrialisation to plants based on the supply-oriented model would have eventually halted the process of industrialisation, just as agricultural development was halted for the same reasons: local resources, aside from manpower, were strictly limited in quantity. On the other hand, industries constructed on the demand-oriented model have a productive potential with only two restrictions: entrepreneurial talent and manpower. Since in Israel at that time manpower was abundant, the demand-oriented model clearly ought to have been preferred by the initiators of the process.

Assessment of the Sapir Era

This was not, in fact, the course chosen. Why not? In order to answer that question one must speculate as to the limited understanding of the man in charge of industrialisation policy, Pinhas Sapir, his absolute faith in his own conception of the task entrusted to him and the means of accomplishing it, as well as his inability to see the short life expectancy of most of the plants built on the basis of supply-oriented entrepreneurship. One is still left wondering why Sapir preferred industrialisation according to the criteria of supply-oriented entrepreneurship, when before his very eyes there were two practical examples of industrialisation on the alternative model based on demand — and both highly successful.

One example was the diamond industry. It began with the immigration of a handful of diamond polishers from the Netherlands just before the outbreak of the Second World War. However, workers alone do not make an industry. In order to get ahead and succeed, capital is needed, but, above all, a market is needed for the product. These two factors respond best to what we have defined as demand-oriented enterprise. In the middle 1950s, when Sapir was put in charge of industrial development, the diamond industry had already expanded beyond the few hundred diamond polishers who had reached Palestine on the eve of the war and by that time it was an industry based entirely on foreign markets. The employment and the return it offered for every dollar invested were no smaller than in other industries, and if Sapir had been more imaginative and a bit less set in his thinking, he would have taken the diamond industry as a model for his industrialisation, instead of plywood and textiles.

The second example is even more striking, because it is more general — Jewish industry in Palestine between 1939 and 1945. These were years of feverish expansion; the added value of industry (the net industrial product) rose from I£4,020 to I£29,800. Corrected for inflation which had virtually trebled in the six years, the net industrial product rose from I£4 million to nearly I£10 million, or by nearly 150 per cent. At the same time the number of workers employed in industry rose from 40,000 to 45,000.[3]

These figures are highly instructive in that, first, the development they describe was achieved with minimal assistance from either the mandatory government or Zionist institutions and second, they provide a perfect example of demand-oriented industrialisation. The years from 1939 to 1945 were war years, and the industrial development was the product of special circumstances which created a sellers' market because of the scarcity of transport and a vigorous institutional demand for supplies for the troops stationed in the region. But viewed from the perspective of the forty intervening years, Jewish industry then appears to have demonstrated marvellous alertness and adaptiveness. It turned itself into the major industrial supplier for the regional war effort, and did so with equipment that was not particularly modern or sophisticated, and exploiting manpower of relatively poor quality because of the widespread conscription of men and women into the British army and the Palmach, an arm of the Jewish defence organisation, the Haganah. This was a sterling example of demand-oriented entrepreneurship in a situation calling for the rapid expansion of industrial capacity — all of which was done, as we noted, without planned assistance from the government. Admittedly , the increase in production, unequalled even during the years of Israel's most rapid industrial expansion, took place under cost-plus conditions and in the absence of effective competition. But even if we take account of the special circumstances of a congenial sellers' market, the example proves the power of demand-oriented industrialisation, provided that entrepreneurial potential exists, as it apparently did in the *Yishuv*. However, once the special challenge of the war passed, this entrepreneurial potential went underground; and when Sapir and the bureaucratic planners of the State of Israel took up industrial development on the formula of the Jewish Agency Settlement Department, they burrowed even deeper, as if they had gone into extended hibernation.

This is the place for a remark which cannot be supported statistically, but which fits in with what has since occurred and with what is known about the talents, possibly hereditary, of the Jewish people. The demand-oriented entrepreneur is first and foremost a trader, in the sense that he is endowed with an ability to sniff out a shortage, in other words, a market. The organisation of supply is secondary in the scheme of bringing together the need to buy with the ability to supply. This is especially true when the demand is not localised, in other words, not limited to a narrow geographical area. Commerce and, similarly, demand-oriented enterprise works well in an international marketplace where, even if there are barriers, they are penetrable. This condition, the ability to discover demand, like the other, that it had to be found in the tenders of the civil and military authorities responsible for large parts of Asia and Africa, existed during the Second World War; the Jewish industrialist-entrepreneur moved in a field of activity extending throughout the Middle East. The Biblical story of Joseph in Egypt illustrates this situation.

The key lay in deciphering Pharaoh's dream and discovering future demand — international demand, incidentally; the actual storing up of the grain for long-term marketing could safely be left in the hands of the pharaonic bureaucracy.

The question remains, why was no lesson learned from these two examples? In a monograph written during the 1960s by Moshe Mandelbaum, then an official in the Ministry of Commerce and Industry and later the Governor of the Bank of Israel, Ian Mikardo, a British MP and an industrial expert, is quoted as complaining that the Israeli industrialist (in the middle 1950s) was essentially a merchant, and as such he believed he knew everything, whereas the industrialist must be aware of his lack of knowledge, on the one hand, and of the need to consult with other people, on the other. Mikardo was talking to civil servants who, true to type, tended to think they knew best what systems to adopt and what goals to pursue in establishing or expanding industry, which explains the basic flaws built into industry during the Sapir period. Decades were to pass before Israeli industry eliminated these flaws and became a productive sector in which the typical manufacturing firm — as opposed to the white elephants of heavy industry, metals, and chemicals — was the product of demand-oriented entrepreneurship.

The Importance of Exports

> Unless definite policies are adopted to change the relative structure of the economy's production in terms of import substitutes and exports, the economy will . . . be in danger of failing to exploit its growing GNP [the most comprehensive index of the economy's productivity] for the purpose of increasing its degree of economic independence.[4]

In that somewhat complex sentence, Professor Dan Patinkin of the Hebrew University, the teacher and spiritual mentor of most of the senior economists in the public service, summarises the lessons of his book, *The Israeli Economy, The First Decade* published in 1967.[4] The sentence contains a prophetic element, which remains true to this day. Only the dimensions of the problem have changed; in essence it remains just as it was when Patinkin completed his manuscript. The first great economic crisis demonstrated the truth of his conclusion, and, incidentally, clarified the questionable nature of industrialisation in the Sapir mode for people who understood such matters.

However, something needs to be added to Professor Patinkin's summary. Economic viability depended on the ability to produce more import substitutes and goods destined for foreign markets, and so did employment and economic activity in general. As became clear in the mid-1960s, and as is being confirmed once again at the time of writing, without an increase in exports there was no way then, nor is there today, of maintaining, let alone expanding, either economic activity or employment.

Around the beginning of the 1960s unemployment ceased to be a serious economic problem. The daily average of unemployment was about 4,000, as against 850,000 employed workers, i.e. less than five per cent. Considering the composition of the adult population, and the relatively high rates of chronic illness and illiteracy which characterised it, this was a negligible percentage. The relationship between employed and unemployed embodied the basic problem of the Israeli economy: employment and its expansion — for at that time the working population was growing at a rate of between three and five per cent annually — depended on one of two factors, increased import of capital, i.e. loans or unilateral transfers from abroad, and increased exports. The devaluation carried out by the government in 1962 after sharp internal discussions — Pinhas Sapir was one of its strongest opponents, although he did not deny the need to encourage exports, but objected to attaining that end by means of a devaluation — is evidence of the growing awareness of the marketability of Israeli products as a necessary condition for achieving the threefold aim of productivisation, full employment, and a rising standard of living.

Two facts illustrate the extent of the problem: in 1960 total exports of goods and services came to 14 per cent of GNP; by 1962 it reached 21 per cent. The more exports grew, the greater their importance as a source of employment. The maintenance of growth therefore necessitated increased exports to pay for the imports on which the expansion of the domestic market depended; borrowing abroad (in the absence of sufficient exports) was not sufficiently controllable to sustain economic policy. The pound was devalued with the aim of encouraging exports. But this step, though considered a radical one at the time, was not very effective; the proportion of exports in GNP stuck at around 21–22 per cent.

An attempt has been made to explain the static proportion of exports by what have been defined above as the Israeli rules of the game. Any rise in the cost of living causes a parallel increase in the costs of production because of the cost of living allowances; and increased production costs cancel the improvement in the ability to compete in foreign markets brought about by the devaluation. This explanation is correct, especially since Israel had been industrialised — and the majority of exports were industrial as early as the beginning of the 1960s — according to the supply-oriented model. In other words, a significant proportion of its exports (excluding diamonds) consisted essentially of the export of wages, and consequently their competitiveness was disproportionately affected by wage increases. Because of this characteristic of the economy, the planners were confronted with a problem similar to the one that plagued those in charge of economic policy in Britain. Any increase in economic activity brought about an increase in domestic costs; exports decreased while imports grew; hence the need arose to reduce costs either by reducing employment or by devaluation; and so on and so on. This is the notorious stop-go cycle, and anyone trapped in it is condemned to keep running on the same spot, with yo-yo-like swings between booms and slumps. In 1965 Israel reached a point in its economic development where it was in real danger of being trapped in a stop-go circle. Exports, although they had been growing steadily for some time, were fated to slow down, owing to the increase in relative money wages. Had industrialisation followed a demand-oriented pattern, i.e. one less affected by relative levels of wages, exports could have gone on increasing notwithstanding rising wages.

Since the potential for industrial exports, other than diamonds, was subject to the limitations inherent in the supply-oriented model, the government sought to encourage them by subsidising production. This gave rise to a constantly growing burden on the government budget. Exports of the textile and garment industry in 1966 may serve as an example of the type of situation liable to emerge from a combination of supply-oriented industrialisation and encouragement of exports through subsidisation. The added value (i.e. the export value less the costs of imported inputs) was $25 million that year, or I£75 million according to the rate of exchange at the time; but the proportion of subsidies in that sector was around I£20 million, almost a third. This excessive rate of subsidisation showed that the policy of industrialisation then being implemented was heading for a dead end.

Official accounts of the major decline in economic activity which took place in 1966 attribute it to the government's decision to slow the pace of public housing construction, because of the slowdown in immigration. Since the construction industry, including its suppliers, was a major force in the economy, this had a considerable depressive effect on other industries. This official description, presented in Sapir's budget speech, in which he set out the arguments in support of the steps the government was about to take, and replicated in the Bank of Israel's Report of 1966 analysing the trends of the government's economic policy and its potential results, was correct, but only as far as it went. The cause of the slowdown was the failure of an economy which operated mainly on the supply-oriented model of industrialisation, and its inability to locate foreign demand sufficient to provide employment for those who were left without work because of a lag in immigration. Thus, according to the official description, what came to light was the economy's inability to react to shifts in demand, although the range of fluctuation did not exceed 1.5–2 per cent of GNP. A comparison of this inability with the flexibility and energy with which the economy, though equipped with a much poorer and more primitive productive apparatus, responded to the challenge of industrialisation during the Second World War only serves to emphasise the systemic weakness built into the economy during Sapir's period of office. During the state's first decade industry did create employment — but employment that was unstable from the start.

The dilemma which then emerged dogged the Israeli economy from the first steps in industrialisation. If the authorities were to reduce wages this would deepen the recession by weakening demand in the local market (quite apart from arousing the opposition of the workers, about which the government was particularly sensitive at the time). But industry based on the export of wages could not expand production for foreign markets, except by tying wages to productivity, and this, because of the nature of the labour force, was not particularly high in international terms.

This is an appropriate place to compare the reactions of the Mapai government to the economic realities in 1966, with those of the Likud Government under Finance Minister Yoram Aridor. Despite the criticisms levelled against them at the time and since, Sapir and his colleagues understood what financial responsibility, including international financial responsibility, meant. When demand slackened and costs continued to rise, the Eshkol Government — unique in Israel's history in being headed by a man with an economic background — reacted by deflating the economy, with the aim of breaking the thrust of rising costs. The action was justified by unwillingness to increase the trade deficit, the inevitable outcome of a government policy aimed at taking up the slack in domestic demand. This policy was the direct opposite of the steps taken by Yoram Aridor after the 1981 elections. In a rather similar situation, he inflated domestic demand by increasing the budget deficit, financed mostly by short-term loans from the international financial community. The results: in 1966 Pinhas Sapir achieved a 15 per cent decrease in the trade deficit, from $535 million to $452 million, in return for the additional unemployment of 40,000 workers; Yoram Aridor maintained full employment, but the trade deficit shot up from $1.4 billion in 1981 to $2.1 billion in 1982, an increase of about 50 per cent.

The blows that fell on the economy in the early 1960s — the devaluation of 1962, the beginning of the slowdown in 1965, and the recession of 1966 — indicate increasingly serious disruptions in the economic system which had evolved since the establishment of the state. The emergence of serious problems in the economy coincided with the process of political disintegration to which the ruling party and its leadership were subject. Whether there was a connection between the two processes, apart from their simultaneity, and what the nature of that connection might have been, if there was one, is a question for which we have no final answer. It seems probable that sooner or later the faulty functioning of the economy ought to have led people to draw conclusions regarding the political system. However, there was no sooner or later here; the two processes occurred simultaneously. The economic and political systems, guided by members of the same party (and in many cases the same men), ceased functioning efficiently at the same time. And to the extent that the Six Day War, which broke out in June 1967, could be said to have rescued the Mapai government and its representatives from the results of a process of disorientation and collapse to which they had long been subject, the same thing can be said about the economic leadership.

After the Six Day War

In the aftermath of the war and victory, the climate changed and so did the conditions which had applied during the recession and before it. There was also a change in the approach to the subject of industrialisation, among other things because Pinhas Sapir relinquished for a certain time the day-to-day management of economic policy. The government withdrew from industrial entrepreneurship. On the other hand, in a manner recalling the events of the Second World War, the government became an important source of demand. Thus, for example, in 1966 the defence establishment spent 64 million sheqels (in constant 1964 prices) on goods and services (including wages) in the local market: between 1967 and 1973 it spent a total of 1.6 billion sheqels, or 229 million annually, three and a half times what it had spent before the war. The defence establishment created a local market, mostly for technologically advanced products, thus creating an atmosphere favourable to demand-oriented entrepreneurship. Firms supplying the military became the example imitated by other industrial entrepreneurs. Others began to view the local civilian market as both limited and unstable; they therefore deliberately oriented their businesses towards potential markets either wholly or partially abroad. Thus many entrepreneurs increasingly abandoned the supply-oriented model of industry for a demand-oriented alternative. Today it would be difficult to find an industrial entrepreneur worth his salt who did not base his planning on the identification of a market, either domestic or foreign, and an estimate of its size. The rest depends on what the entrepreneur finds. One result of the change described here is that today we hear much less than in the past of wages as the cost factor interfering with exports. Instead, critical attention is given by the entrepreneur to other costs, such as interest rates — an entrepreneurial cost *par excellence*.

Ideologies

One upshot of the change in the national agenda following the Six Day War was the deproductivisation of Israel. The term 'deproductivisation' is not very precise. In public usage it is meant to describe what happens when workers leave agriculture, manufacturing, or construction for employment in the service sector; used in this fashion, the term implies a value judgment, suggesting, among other things, that the overall efficiency of the economy is diminished when it loses a construction worker and gains a lecturer in electrical engineering. The analytical value of the term is therefore somewhat doubtful. Nevertheless, changes did take place for which the term may be deemed appropriate. First the effect in terms of ideology must be described.

One of the main tasks faced by the national leadership during Israel's first decade was to make the rapidly growing population productive. This was connected in the minds of the leaders with the Zionist goal of inverting the employment pyramid of the Jewish people in the diaspora and placing it on its base. The people's redemption for exile was meant to proceed hand in hand with its redemption from its earlier way of life, including redemption from insubstantial occupations such as trading, begging and the like. It is a mistake to think that utilitarian considerations alone guided the national leadership in their obsessive emphasis on the moral value of labour. Retrospectively it can be seen that in many cases jobs were created which should not have been, and that it would have been better to post the worker a cheque signed by the state comptroller. The same applies to the owners of the firms in which the worker was employed. The reason that such a procedure was inconceivable, except in economic theory, is to be found in the view of the economic leadership, which did not regard economic activity as merely a way of producing and distributing goods and services, but rather as a means of removing historical distortions that had undermined the structure of Jewish society and the character of the individual Jew.

In the aftermath of the Six Day War, work as a value was abandoned along with other values, most of them inherited from the period of the Mandate, which had moulded the cultural profile of Israeli society from 1948 onwards. Ministers no longer spoke of work as an independent value, nor did cultural leaders, and even popular songs no longer dealt with it. The change became fully apparent in the late 1970s, with the discovery of poverty by the Israeli people and their elected and administrative bodies and its promotion to the status of a social problem of the first order. During the first decade and a half, perhaps the first two decades, of the state, as we saw in Chapter 2, the recognised social dichotomy, the axis around which the struggle for the distribution of national income revolved, was the traditional socialist division between boss and worker, or, in more neutral terms, employer and employee. Then, strongly influenced by the model imported from the United States, Israel also adopted the fashionable social division between the rich and the poor, rather than between employers and employees. According to the new model, a rich person is someone who enjoys the products of the affluent society to a satisfactory degree or in excess. A poor person is someone whose share is set at a minimum called the poverty line or even falls short of it. The terminology as well as the reality embodied in this second dichotomy is much murkier than the previous one. But since, according to the new fashion, class struggle was seen to be an antiquated concept, and since the proponents of the new terminology could point to the absurdity of placing a salaried bank manager on one side of the social barrier and a carpenter employing three workers on the other, it was an easy matter for many people to replace the old pattern of social struggle by the new, fashionable one. Among those who exchanged the old for the new were, rather surprisingly, the General Secretaries of the Histadrut, like Yitzhak Ben-Aharon and, afterwards, Yeruhaom Meshel, who began to discuss poverty and take up positions in favour of the poor.

The new ideas were bound up not only with the use of terminology invented by American sociologists, but also with the adoption of a different value system. A worker who does not earn a decent living is a victim of exploitation, the mechanism of which was thoroughly explained by Karl Marx and his disciples. To do battle against exploitation, workers were called upon to organise in unions and parties, their demands for an improved standard of living being based on the proposition that their labour was worth more than the employers paid for it. In other words, it was claimed that an exchange of work in return for a wage had been deliberately distorted by those wielding sufficient socio-political power to do so. The contrast between rich and poor is something quite different. The rich person — 'the bad guy' in the new scheme — might actually be receiving his due share of the national income according to criteria of productivity or entrepreneurship, in other words, the standard economic criteria. The poor person, on the other hand, might be poor because he lacks education, because of illness, chronic drunkenness, or drug addiction, or simply because he prefers idleness to work; in other words, his poverty might be economically justified. However, it is sufficient for a person to be rich for society to be justified in taking away a portion of his wealth.

Correspondingly, it is sufficient for a person to be poor for him to claim public assistance financed by tax monies collected from those defined as rich, according to standards set by the proponents of the new social fashion and under pressure from them.

As has been mentioned, during the first years of the state practical arguments in favour of productivisation were stressed: the productive industries, whose development and advancement were acknowledged to be a necessary condition for the existence of a self-sustaining state, needed workers. The large number of potential labourers, on the one hand, and the productive processes dictated by the plentiful labour supply, on the other, complemented each other harmoniously. However, during the early 1960s a certain surplus in labour supply began to be felt: in the recession of 1966 that surplus manifested itself in circumstances that aroused concern. After the 1967 victory the surplus disappeared, and a shortage of labour began to make its appearance: it was supplied by drawing from the population reserves of the occupied territories. However, the shortage was transient, concentrated in a few sectors (construction and various types of services) and, to an extent, artificial because of the feverish increase in demand for labour in the defence system. It soon became clear to anyone who cared to look beneath the surface, that what were known as the productive sectors of the economy had absorbed few workers, or at any rate did not absorb them in sufficient numbers to supply employment for every potential job-seeker. Thus in 1970, out of close on 950,000 civilian employees, 430,000 worked in agriculture, mineral extraction, industry (including electricity and water), or construction, i.e. approximately 45 per cent. In 1982 the civilian labour force numbered about 1.3 million, of whom 530,000 were employed in the aforementioned areas, i.e. 41 per cent. In other words, in twelve years only 100,000 workers were absorbed in the primary and secondary sectors of the economy, out of the 350,000 added in all areas of the civilian economy. This phenomenon is attributable to several causes operating simultaneously: for the purpose of the present discussion it is sufficient to note that new technology, especially in agriculture and manufacturing, and also in construction to some extent, led to a relative reduction in demand for labour in those areas. And since the entire economy was being reorganised on the pattern of demand-oriented enterprise, there was no official interest or pressure to employ workers in the primary and secondary sectors anyway.

In 1971 there were one million people in the civilian work force. Ten years later, in 1981, their number reached 1.28 million. Table 5.1 illustrates the process of deproductivisation: the fastest growth during the decade between 1971 and 1981 occurred in the financial services: the number employed doubled in absolute terms, and the branch rose from the second-to-last to the fifth place. The other branch in which the total number of workers increased rapidly was the public services, whose share of employment grew from approximately 24 per cent to nearly 30 per cent. In contrast, the percentage share of industry fell, although in absolute terms it absorbed close on 60,000 new workers; in agriculture and construction the decline was absolute as well as relative. It would be no exaggeration to say that the decade between 1971 and 1981 was a decade of bankers, stock-brokers, and bureaucrats in public service. Two further comments are in order: (i) the change began under Labour and continued at an accelerated pace under the Likud, and (ii) this turn of events was out of keeping, to put it mildly, with the vision of the fathers of Zionism, who had wished to reverse the Jewish employment pyramid. Perhaps a third comment might be ventured: of all branches of commerce, trading in financial paper is the most insubstantial and best deserving the derisory Yiddish appellation of *luftgeheftn* 'air business'. But this was precisely the branch of commerce which did especially well during the decade under discussion.

Some commentators have suggested that what occurred in the Israeli economy at that time was part of the process of normalisation: the present employment structure of Israel is similar to that in other developed industrial countries, including the United States;

Table 5.1 Employment in Various Branches of the Economy 1971–81

	1971 (thousands)	%	1981 (thousands)	%
Agriculture	85	8.5	77	6
Industry	240	24.1	298	23.2
Electricity and Water	11	1.1	14	1.1
Construction	89	8.9	79	6.1
Commerce, Hotels	127	12.7	152	11.9
Transportation	74	7.4	85	6.6
Finance	57	5.7	111	8.8
Public Services	242	24.3	381	29.7
Personal Services	72	7.3	74	5.7

further, this similarity is no coincidence but rather the product of economic forces typical of modern economies in the post-industrial age. However, whereas the new employment structures in the wealthy industrial states were built on a firm foundation in terms of variety of supply and a high level of productivity, this was not the case in Israel. In fact, when comparing Israel to the industrial nations, the similarity in their employment structure ought to arouse surprise and concern.

In conclusion, it may be said that by the beginning of the fourth decade of the State of Israel the foundations of a modern economy possessing considerable competitive ability were in place. But a large bureaucracy, which has kept growing at a fast pace even during the rule of a party traditionally opposed to big government, hangs round the neck of the economy like a millstone. There is also a growing welfare burden. These impediments, in addition to Israel's disproportionately large defence burden, have inevitably slowed down the drive toward self-sustaining growth.

The Likud Upheaval

One party's tenure of power for decades necessarily deprives the opposition of government experience and their inexperience affects the functioning of the new leaders adversely when they assume senior ministerial posts. When the Likud took over in 1977 its leadership had few people with practical economic experience — apart from what could be acquired in the Knesset committees dealing with economic matters. Moreover, it also lacked men with the sort of expertise, acquired either by study or by managing large companies or government corporations, which gives one a broad perspective on the national economy. In other words, the men put in charge of the economic management of the country were essentially amateurs, and they have remained so to this day. Although the then Minister of Finance, Yoram Aridor, had a better formal education than any of his predecessors, the difference between the practical experience of the Likud ministers in the economic sphere and in the political and military field, is noteworthy. Not only had Menachem Begin served as a minister, albeit without portfolio, in the Eshkol and Meir Governments of 1967–70, and therefore witnessed the decision-making process of government and participated in it to a certain extent, but he also strengthened the political scope of his government by co-opting Moshe Dayan as Minister of Foreign Affairs, and its military side by including Generals Weitzmann and Sharon. In contrast, the first Begin Government did not include a single man with experience of economic management at any senior level. The Finance Minister, Simha Ehrlich, and the Minister of Commerce and Industry, Yigael Horowitz, had experience and professional expertise befitting managers of small or middle-sized economic enterprises; moreover, they had no public standing as economists. This affected both their status within the government and their ability to execute the policies they advocated.

It would have been inconceivable that the Likud, coming to power after twenty-nine years in opposition, should abstain from innovation in economic policy. It was especially inconceivable that Liberal Party activists within the Likud should have held back, for they had an economic message of their own: they stood for a market economy, liberated from the despotism of governmental bureaucracy. Moreover, the Liberals saw that their partner, Herut, was doing as it pleased in matters of foreign and defence policy. The impulse to act, and to act in dramatic fashion, grew stronger until the Liberal economic ministers could no longer restrain it. This was the background to the economic upheaval that took place in October 1977. Amateurism and showmanship joined forces in the hasty formulation of policy, and even more so in its hasty execution. The initiators of the new economic policy did not foresee the difficulties to which it would give rise. When he announced the new policy, Simha Ehrlich said he had suffered sleepless nights before deciding on it; with unexpected foresight, he added, 'I have taken a weighty responsibility upon myself and risked my political future'.[5] However, it turned out that loss of sleep offers no protection against errors deriving from ignorance and inexperience.

At the end of 1977 the Israeli economy was adrift. The gross business product (i.e. the GNP less the value of government activities) had grown by only one per cent (all the statistics presented here are set in constant prices) as compared with 1976: but exports had grown by almost 12 per cent. In such circumstances, while the economy contained reserve manpower, mainly the underemployed, the government should have made a particular effort to promote exports and to eliminate, once and for all, the dependence of the producers, particularly the industrial producers, on the local market. In fact, the government did two things: it abolished exchange control without anticipating how the change, essentially a technical one, would affect imports and exports; and then, starting in 1978, it acted energetically to stimulate local demand, thus tempting industry to try its luck in the local market. Apparently the government based its decisions on the assumption that free movement in foreign exchange would cause a fall in the value of the sheqel and thus increase export opportunities. In fact, dollars flowed into the Israeli banking system, having the opposite effect to what was desired. Long months passed before the authorities made the necessary adjustment. In any case, the first effect of the upheaval was to halt exports and encourage imports. Table 5.2 shows some of the results.

The rate of growth in private consumption almost doubled: the growth of exports was halved; and imports, which had declined by 2 per cent in 1976–7, increased by 9 per cent. Another change also took place, which, in later years, was severely to harm the economy: inflation accelerated very rapidly, as is shown in Table 5.3.

Floating the currency, that is, letting supply and demand set the rate of exchange in the financial market, was a reasonable step in itself, the more so as under the last Labour government a system of creeping devaluation had already been adopted. However, the timing was faulty: the currency should have been devalued after the export industries had achieved independence from the local economy, let us say, after two years of intense promotion of exports, once they had become a leading factor in economic growth. Moreover, the floating of the shequel, even at the time when it was done, could have achieved the desired results, if it had been accompanied by monetary and budgetary policies designed to prevent the rise in domestic demand. But the necessary restraints were not imposed: the Liberals in the Likud missed an opportunity which is

Table 5.2 Changes in Economic Indicators 1976–8

	1976	1977 %	1978 %
Private Consumption	—	+4	+7
Exports	—	+12	+6
Imports	—	−2	+9

Table 5.3 Average Annual Inflation Rates (%)

1968–70	1971–3	1974–7	1978	1979	1980	1981	1982
3	15	36	51	78	128.7	124.1	118.5

unlikely to return soon, if ever, to derive permanent economic benefit from the improved competitiveness of certain branches of Israeli industry following the 1967 war.

A question arises here: was it only because of his lack of professional knowledge that Simha Ehrlich missed his big opportunity, or were there deeper causes, inherent in his economic philosophy, or the collective character of the Liberal Party? Later on, we shall see that if it was the result of a philosophy or a collective characteristic, they were not peculiar to the Liberals. Like them, the Herut party was marked by what must be termed economic permissiveness. Menachem Begin used to declare that he wanted to do well by the people. His first government acted on this precept, and so did his second one, but with a vengeance. Of the three finance ministers who served under Begin, only one wanted to impose economic austerity: Yigael Horowitz, a former member of Mapai. The other two, Simha Ehrlich and Yoram Aridor, so different from each other in personality, in party origins, and in formal economic training, turned out to be finance ministers who swam with the tide and who refrained from imposing policies likely to encounter public resistance.

The Bank of Israel Report of 1979 described the economy as suffering from excess demand fuelled by government spending, even though the government could point to a compensatory achievement: GNP grew by 5 per cent. However, imports increased from $10.2 billion to $12 billion, and exports only grew from $7 to $8.4 billion. The growing gap in the balance of payments apparently scared the political leaders: Ehrlich was forced to resign, and Yigael Horowitz was appointed in his place. He imitated his predecessor once removed, Yehoshua Rabinowitz, and introduced a deflationary policy. He cut subsidies, restricted the expansion of the money supply, and appealed to the public, in a tearful voice and with an expression presaging disaster, calling for restraint, for making do with less, and, above all, for saving dollars. It soon became clear that he was a foreign element in the Likud and, apart from his being a fervent believer in the integrity of the Land of Israel, was quite unlike his ministerial colleagues in his policies, and even more in his willingness to demand sweat and tears from the public.

So, after serving as Minister of Finance for less than a year, he was invited by his colleagues to quit, to no small degree because they were apprehensive that by telling the truth about the economic chaos he had inherited from his predecessor, and even more his vigorous effort to put the economy in some order, he would cause the Likud to lose the elections. After Horowitz's dismissal, they sought a successor after their own hearts and came up with Yoram Aridor. In no time he proved to be the find of the year, an election year, as it happened. Under his leadership the Israeli people set out on an economic bonanza unprecedented in the three decades since the establishment of the state: in real terms private consumption increased in the election year of 1981 by 10.5 per cent.

The Likud again won a plurality of seats, and there was not a single commentator who failed to attribute the lion's share in that victory to Yoram Aridor. But the cynics were wrong: Aridor had not instituted election year policies. He sincerely believed, apparently trusting the opinions of charlatans gathered around him in the administration of the Treasury, that it was possible to beat inflation by government subsidies, and that increasing balance of payments deficits were an annoyance but not a matter which ought to concern economic policy makers unduly. His greatest achievement was in disguising the theoretical and practical bankruptcy of his economic policies until mid-1983. He might not actually have had to admit his failure, had he not become involved in a side issue, the doctors' strike, from which he retreated badly mauled.

It is impossible to conclude this review of the Likud era in the Israeli economy without mentioning the appearance of the stock market speculator. The Tel Aviv Stock Exchange is as old as the state, and it had known steep rises in the mid-1960s. At that time some people made big, non-taxable, capital gains. But the speculator as a main actor in the economy and stock market speculation as a full-time occupation, something for which many abandoned their regular employment or business, was a novel development. By late 1982 stock market speculation had become a kind of popular sport; it was estimated that at that time more than a million people owned stocks or shares in mutual funds, and in most cases they bought securities in order to make capital gains through frequent purchases and sales. With the appearance of the stockholder, albeit in somewhat flawed form, the process of adapting the Israeli economy to the pattern common to all advanced industrial economies was complete. Henceforth anyone wishing to undo the process, either in response to external pressures or for ideological reasons, has to be aware that it is no longer possible to resort to the methods of economic management applied in the

1960s, not least because of this addition to the cast of players on the stage.

Notes

1. Robert Nathan, Oscar Gass and Daniel Kramer, *Palestine, Problem and Promise* (Public Affairs Press, Washington, D. C., 1946).

2. Verbal communication with the author.

3. These figures are taken from Robert Shershewski, *The Structure of the Jewish Economy in Palestine* (Hebrew) (Maurice Falk Institute for Economic Research, Jerusalem, 1968).

4. Don Patinkin, *The Israeli Economy, The First Decade* (Maurice Falk Institute for Economic Research, Jerusalem, 1967).

5. *Haaretz*, 30 October 1977.

6 TOWARDS THE NEXT CHANGEOVER

Even before Menachem Begin shocked his colleagues by announcing that he intended to resign, there had been clear signs of a crisis brewing within the Likud and the Herut Movement. Rather naturally it became most visible in the two areas where Begin's second government took its prime initiatives: in Lebanon and in economic policy. However, there is good reason to believe that an existential crisis was underlying surface events. Seventeen years after the formation and adoption of the national agenda of which the Likud was the outstanding proponent and more than seven years after the Knesset elections that brought the changeover in government the pendulum had begun to swing in the opposite direction.

The swing may be said to have started with the elections which took place in July 1984 — or possibly even earlier, in the autumn of 1983, with the new leader of the Likud, Yitzhak Shamir, inviting the head of the Labour opposition to join him in a Government of National Unity. On the face of it, this initiative proved a failure, but it did indicate a loss of faith by Likud leaders in their ability to carry on as before. Thus, it paved the way for Shimon Peres to force the holding of elections about a year and a half before the normal term.

The elections did not produce a winner; but they did produce a clear loser, namely the Likud, which forfeited about 15 per cent of its parliamentary strength. More importantly, Likud came in second, behind Labour, in the private race between the two major parties, and thus was unable to scrape together a majority, however thin, to form a government under its own leadership. The details of the Likud leader's struggle against the arithmetic of the election results and its inevitable outcome are not really important. What was important was the formation of a national coalition with Shimon Peres at its head. Peres was accorded a two-year term of office; under the deal, he was to hand over to Shamir for the second half of the four-year legislative term. But in the first half the Labour-Likud coalition is functioning as a Labour government, as it were. This can be seen clearly in the virtual cessation of new settlements in the administered territories, in the rapid pull-out from

138

Lebanon, in the general shape of the economic austerity programme started in the summer of 1985, and in the receptive attitude to peace initiatives launched by President Mubarak of Egypt and King Hussein of Jordan.

It is vain to speculate on the outcome of the 1984 elections, had Labour conducted them in a more combative fashion, that is, if a more strenuous effort had been made to draw a clearer line dividing Labour policies from those of the Likud. Equally vain is speculation on whether the Likud has lost its leadership position merely for the time being, owing to its mismanagement of the nation's business in the years 1982–4, or whether this is a sign of a long-term shift in the political trend. But two points ought to be mentioned here which bear on the main thesis offered in this book: the change occurred against a background of confident predictions by Israeli psephologists that the Likud had in fact become the long-term majority party, and polls taken since the elections show a reasonably clear Labour lead. Add to this the continued disarray in the Likud leadership, both personal and political, and the conclusion seems to be that the Likud as the leading force in government is on the way out.

Only the coming years, however, will conclusively tell whether history will repeat itself, that is, whether the Likud, like Mapai from 1967 to 1977, will adopt a national agenda essentially alien to it but one put into practice, at least partially, under a Likud-led coalition; or whether a different government will come into existence to implement a new national agenda to which it is committed.

We have already said that once the national agenda with which Mapai was identified had been accomplished, the party should have given way to another leading party in the elections of 1961, or, at the very latest, in 1965. However, poor organisation and lack of self-confidence prevented the opposition — particularly the Herut-Liberal bloc which arose before the 1965 elections — from clearly asking the public to draw the proper conclusions from Mapai's programmatic exhaustion and to replace it with a government offering a substantially different vision and programme. Israel therefore continued to stagnate until the war in 1967; after it, and as a result of it, an alternative national agenda took shape rapidly but, by reason of historical chance — chiefly Moshe Dayan's personality — Mapai came to execute it and continued to wield power and enjoy its perquisites.

Looking at these events analytically, one can distinguish between those over which no control was exerted and those which were produced by conscious decisions made by the party leaderships in response to a given set of events. Both Herut and the General Zionists party drew the right conclusions from the clear signs of decline in Mapai's authority, but co-operation between the two parties aimed at replacing Mapai and basing their policies on an alternative national agenda was delayed because of the hopes nurtured by the General Zionists — which proved to be vain — that they could form a coalition with Mapai. Here too a conscious decision was made: the General Zionists entered into partnership with the Progressives to create an atmosphere conducive to the renewal of the coalition with Mapai similar to the one which had existed in the early 1950s. This decision indicated that Yosef Sapir and his comrades lacked confidence in their ability to emerge victorious from a confrontation with Mapai, and perhaps also their unwillingness to identify with the Land of Israel plank in the Herut platform. However, by the time of the 1965 elections it had become clear to the General Zionists that Mapai had blocked the way to co-operation with them. Once again a conscious decision was taken: they split from the Progressives and entered into an alliance with Herut. It was, however, a hesitant alliance. The public had good reason not to place excessive faith in its pretensions to govern and its declared programme. The next important decisions were taken by Mapai, particularly in response to the pressure of the events of the Six Day War: namely, the cooption of Dayan, which implied the adoption of a national agenda different from their own and alien to their views.

Today conditions are different: Likud is in the doldrums, there is a Labour Prime Minister who is very much in charge and Labour Ministers are quite comfortable in their jobs. However, as mentioned earlier, events can turn either way. The outcome depends on the decisions of the party leaderships, either to respond to grassroots pressures for a change or to make a deliberate attempt to carry on with the nationalist and expansionist agenda which has guided the national leadership since 1967. For some time, perhaps several years, such an attempt could well succeed. But sooner or later, the gap between needs as perceived by the public and the political elites, and the policies actually implemented on the basis of a national agenda which no longer represents the popular will, must lead to a crisis: then its replacement will be unavoidable (as was the case after the Six Day War). Even when a crisis of this sort leads to the replacement, not of one item or another in the policies of the government, but a shift of the entire set of co-ordinates of national policy, it is possible — as we learned from the example of 1966 — for the hard shell of the regime, which was identified with the previous national agenda, to remain intact, and only its substance to be replaced by something different as required by the new situation. Whether and how such a thing happens depends on decisions made by the party leaderships. In principle it can be said that the more the party seeking to make a change is identified unequivocally with an alternative national agenda — and this depends on the clarity of the identification, the definition of goals, and on their intellectual underpinning — the better its chances of replacing the government. In other words, clarity and the will to confront are at a premium for the opposition at a time when the continued existence of a national agenda is in the balance. This characteristic should be emphasised because the politics of a democracy — possibly of any sort of regime — tend toward the dead centre, at which public debate seldom goes beyond mere details about which decisions can be taken in routine discussions held in the political establishment, the Knesset and party headquarters.

The Crisis in Likud

Menachem Begin's two governments never functioned harmoniously, and from the late summer of 1982 until the premier's announcement of his wish to resign, the government was virtually paralysed. At first glance the main reason for the paralysis appears to lie in the events following the IDF's penetration of West Beirut, more precisely, the massacre in the Palestinian refugee camps. But more careful scrutiny would show that even before these events, the sense of the political community was increasingly that the war in Lebanon was not turning out well. The most decisive evidence for this can be found in the plan put forward by President Reagan for a political settlement in the Middle East, under which the Americans proposed to bring the King of Jordan into the peace process and, with his co-operation, to raise the issue of sovereignty over Judea, Samaria, and the Gaza Strip. Begin rejected the plan out of hand. His rejection showed growing nervous strain and loss of confidence on his part, brought about by the difference between his expectations of the war and its actual results. In any event, after witnessing the outburst of animosity against Israel during the war in Lebanon, the government must have sensed that if such was the reward for a military action, which by that time had left about 500 dead and thousands wounded, in an action, moreover, which was meant to serve US interests, its initiators, Menachem Begin and Ariel Sharon, must have made a bad bargain typical of political amateurs. There was a collapse of faith in what everyone had previously regarded as the Prime Minister's forte: his authority in matters of foreign policy. A vicious circle then began: the collapse of his authority ate into Begin's self-confidence and caused him increasingly to withdraw into himself; his withdrawal damaged what remained of the government's inner unity and its members' confidence in the Prime Minister; this, in turn, caused him to withdraw further into himself; and so on. However, typically for Israeli politics under the Likud, the disappointment over Lebanon, which was generally experienced even in the main governing party, was not given verbal expression: the Likud never held a post-mortem on the war. It did not call its leaders to account, blame anyone, single anyone out for praise, or demand anyone's resignation. Nevertheless, in the wake of a subterranean political process, overlaid by a continued decline in Begin's physical and mental condition, the Likud came to resemble a decapitated body.

From the establishment of the state, Israel had developed a political tradition according to which the operations of government were divided in two: foreign affairs and defence were the province of the Prime Minister, the Minister of Defence, and the Minister of Foreign Affairs; the rest came under the authority of the Minister of Finance. National policy was shaped, except between 1963 and 1969 under Levi Eshkol, by people whose roots were anchored in their political and defence activities. The two governments of Menachem Begin reinforced that tradition. Yoram Aridor was able to exploit the freedom of action granted to him within this framework. Convinced that a magic formula had been revealed to him, whereby it was possible simultaneously to overcome three digit inflation and to maintain full employment and a constantly rising standard of living, he hastened to implement it. What his colleagues and outside observers viewed as a temporary pre-election trick later proved to be an article of faith for the Minister of Finance, which he was set on putting into practice once the Likud returned to power following the 1981 elections.

Even when the war in Lebanon was started, he did not exploit the opportunity to reverse the permissive policies he had instituted. The result, galloping deterioration in the balance of trade and the country's external debt, was not slow in coming. In the summer of 1983 a full-blown crisis developed, brought on by the deterioration in the balance of payments deficit. The most vociferous critics of the Minister of the Finance were his colleagues in the government and fellow-members of his party, but they publicised their doubts as to the validity of Aridor's magic formula only after the sense that it was a fraud had become widespread. Possibly his critics might have delayed their attack even longer if the Minister of Finance had not become embroiled in the doctors' strike. Owing to a tragi-comic misreading of the effect that granting an exceptional pay increase to the doctors would have on wage stability, he adopted an excessively rigid negotiating posture. In any case, the strength of his position and his immunity to criticism within the Cabinet were such that only resounding failure could unseat him. But the mess he had made of things was there for all to see, and although his comrades and colleagues joined in the assault upon him, they were viewed, as members of the same party and government, as equally responsible with the minister upon whom they now vented their anger and frustration.

There were clear indications that not only had the crisis engulfed Menachem Begin's second government because of the disappointing results of the war in Lebanon and the increasingly evident difficulties in the economy administered by Yoram Aridor, but that the national agenda, of which the Likud was the outstanding proponent, had also lost its validity and no longer suited the public's needs. There were signs that expansionist nationalism, the prime characteristic of the Likud agenda, no longer had the mass appeal it had enjoyed in the years prior to Begin's rise to power, or again during the blistering months when foreign leaders antagonistic to Israel were showered with abuse, when Syrian helicopters were shot down in Lebanon, and when the nuclear reactor in Iraq was destroyed. Various hypotheses could be put forward as to what changed the public attitude. A possible explanation could be that a daily dose of provocative declarations was incompatible with the desire for full enjoyment of the material plenty promised by Aridor's economy, including cheap foreign travel and the plentiful supply of Japanese consumer electronics.

However, it would seem that the war in Lebanon played a particularly important part: it displayed, in television reports straight from the battlefield, what was implicit in Likud's national agenda. The sight of the policies as they were being implemented, in fire and smoke, was brought right into the average Israeli's living room. Pictures of killing and destruction apparently had an effect, just as similar ones had affected Americans in their homes during the war in Vietnam. It was Menachem Begin himself who created the indissoluble link between what the Israelis saw on television and, even more powerfully, what the soldiers experienced on the battlefield, and the boastful words accompanying these pictures like background music. It was *his* war, and the war of his confidants at the time, Ariel Sharon, Raphael Eitan, and the like — and, moreover, Begin had glorified this optional war, one which was not forced upon Israel, as the preferred instrument for his policies. It was the war, not as an abstract action, but as a sequence of distasteful events witnessed by everyone, with its optional character generally understood, which must be assumed to have aroused grave doubts as to the national agenda justifying it.

Additional evidence of growing alienation from the expansionist-nationalist agenda can be seen in the diminished stature of Gush Emunim. The Gush had been one of the heralds of Likud rule and the main agent of its plan for conquering the land by means of settlement, which had been a distinguishing mark of Begin's first term of office. After 1981 Gush Emunim was mainly visible in its attempts to delay, if not to frustrate, the withdrawal from eastern Sinai, and this brought it into head-on collision with its former partners, chiefly Begin himself. In the subsequent confrontation Gush Emunim came out as the loser; since then its actions have been limited to attempts to gain a foothold in Hebron and dig in, and to bloody conflicts in that city and around it. In any event, people stopped singing its praises and waxing enthusiastic over the pioneering spirit burning in the hearts of its members: romanticism — and Messianic fervour too — turned its back on the settlements.

In any case, the entire settlement effort failed to gain mass support. From early 1981 until the time of writing, the number of Jewish residents of Judea, Samaria, and the Gaza Strip (excluding the municipal limits of Jerusalem) increased to almost 30,000, less than one per cent of the Jewish population of Israel, and about two per cent of the Arab population of these regions. The claim that such a marginal demographic change was sufficient to create an irreversible situation is unrealistic: a civilian population of this size is not strong enough to withstand military pressures from the enemy or, consequently, external political pressure.

While many will remember 1982 as the year of the Lebanese War, others may recall it as the year of the stock exchange. It began with a fantastic boom, in which share prices became completely divorced from any economic basis. The end of the year saw the beginning of a prolonged collapse, bringing to light further underlying flaws and distortions and making people doubt the truth and authority of the economic views dominant during Menachem Begin's second term. The Treasury and the other economic offices claimed that things were just fine, but the public was listening to other opinions. The President of the Manufacturers' Association, for example, repeatedly warned that current economic policy would lead to disaster. The public was used to hearing criticism of the government voiced by the opposition or by the heads of the Labour-dominated Histadrut. But criticism coming not only from politically neutral businessmen, but from the very spokesman for economic circles which naturally tended to be close to the ruling party, was an altogether different matter. The doubts created by the war in Lebanon with regard to the correctness of the Likud philosophy and the validity of its response to political and defence problems, were joined by economic doubts: a complete *Weltanschauung* began to collapse in the aftermath of the events of 1982 and 1983.

Even if affairs had been managed properly, Menachem Begin's resignation from the premiership after a period of embarrassing and distressing decline, would have been a severe blow to the Likud. As noted above, the Likud, and more specifically its hard core, the Herut Movement, has no history, merely the biography of its leader. This explains the gravity of the resignation of the man who had embodied the authority and democratic legitimacy of the government just at a time of confusion when the political and economic way had been lost. The Likud was severely damaged. There is no more convincing evidence of its parlous state than the fact that when Begin's successor, Yitzhak Shamir, was called upon to put together a coalition, he showed willingness to include the Labour Party. Shamir had not been enthusiastic about turning to his rival, and nor was his party. But the lack of firm opposition within the Likud to the very idea of partnership showed the extent of the confusion reigning inside the party and the feeling of helplessness which had gripped its leadership. This action recalls what happened to Mapai in its decline: when it had to resolve the quarrel that had broken out among its leaders during the Lavon Affair, it felt obliged to mobilise support from its rivals within the Labour Movement, and even outside it, in the media and the public at large. The very willingness to consider a national coalition (of the sort discussed in the autumn of 1983) in the middle of a parliamentary term was tantamount to a declaration of bankruptcy. It meant that the government, whose main policies were firmly anchored in the Likud precepts, no longer had the strength to offer solutions to the political problems at hand. By turning to the Labour Party, albeit under duress, the Likud showed that it had come to the end of its tether.

The elections held in 1984 demoted the Likud from its position as the leading party but did not eliminate it from the contest. Thus its situation came to resemble, to some extent, that of Mapai, which continued to lead governments even though, from an ideological point of view as well as organisationally, it had been ripe for replacement in the early 1960s. Exhausting the potential for leadership does not necessarily bring about an immediate loss of power. The reasons for Mapai's survival as the leading party in the coalition have already been indicated above: the lack of an ideological alternative, i.e. an alternative leadership which could offer the people a new national agenda and which was capable of governing from an organisational point of view. Historical chance also played its part, as with Gamal Abdul Nasser's mad decision to challenge Israel's right to exist without being prepared to have his challenge taken up, or Moshe Dayan's availability on the margins of Mapai, prepared to return to the fold with ideological baggage marvellously appropriate for the period after the victory. Unforeseen events, and leadership talents at present unknown or unrecognised, may again combine to bring about a Likud revival, despite its having exhausted the national agenda of which it had been the best representative. But as of now, the chances are dim, for Likud not only has to share with Labour the advantages accruing to a government in power, but its position on the nationalist right is being challenged by parties even more militant.

The Likud's national agenda has been taken as far as it will go. Part of it had already been implemented between 1967 and 1977, and the rest was put into effect from then until Menachem Begin's resignation. Labour is now part of the government and will remain so, even if — and this is a big if — and when Peres hands over the premiership to Shamir. The public resources of Labour, including a large and faithful electorate and a 'patriotic' legitimacy conferred on it by its partnership in government with Likud, put it in a strong position in the race for power. However, from a programmatic point of view, the party's features are — still — blurred. This was clearly shown during the election campaign and since. It takes a skilled observer to make out its programmatic features, for instance in the actions of its Cabinet Ministers, except for the more doveish cast of their foreign policy attitudes and the primacy attaching to full employment in the thinking of the Prime Minister. These are still a far cry, however, from constituting a new national agenda, around which a stable and long-term majority could rally, and which is the necessary and sufficient condition for providing the country with a strong and durable national leadership.

The Two Agendas

Since 1948 two national agendas have guided Israel. One turned inward, towards the absorption of immigration, towards construction and industrialisation; in its outward manifestations, it was minimalist, in other words, satisfied with the territorial basis created during the War of Independence and with the international status befitting a small state at the start of its existence. In 1967 the order was reversed. Territorial expansion, the digestion of the conquests of the Six Day War, and the creation of the status of a regional power were at the centre of the national effort. In domestic affairs the national agenda was characterised by a decline in government initiative. Social initiative became fragmented, passing to individuals, firms, and pressure groups. One can also differentiate between the two agendas in terms of the circumstances of their inception. The 1948 agenda came into being in response to constraints that were a matter of absolute necessity. The demands of absorption and development left the public and the government no choice but to strain every muscle in a supreme effort to consolidate and strengthen the new state by assimilating, albeit in a crude fashion, a new population to the veteran *Yishuv*. In addition, there was military weakness. After the War of Independence there was not a single public body with any standing which actually proposed expanding the borders or improving the political status of the new state by means of force. In contrast, the national agenda which took shape after 1967 was predicated upon the opportunity created by the Six Day War: in other words, it was the product of choice made in the minds of the Israeli public, in response to geographical and political horizons which opened up in dramatic fashion. Now a new national agenda is taking shape, the third since the establishment of the state, again under rigid political and, particularly, economic constraints: and, as dictated by the circumstances of its consolidation, it is likely to be similar in tendency to that of 1948.

It was noted above that the dynamism behind the conquest of the land through settlement has been halted. The general public was not tempted, despite the fortunes spent by the government, to promote it. The belief that Israel had the ability to play the role of a regional power also met with disappointment in Lebanon. To be a regional power means to be able to impose one's will on one's neighbours, largely ignoring external factors, i.e. the great powers. In Lebanon it was proved that, by these standards, Israel is not such a power: it was forced to stop the fighting prematurely, and even its immediate goal, the achievement of a political settlement with Lebanon which guaranteed the permanent removal of the PLO from its territory, seemed to be beyond its grasp. On the positive side, there is the continued military occupation of Judea, Samaria, and the Gaza Strip: in other words, the conquests of 1967 have not been lost (although today their maintenace demands a much greater effort than in the years immediately after the war). A number of settlements were also implanted in these areas, some of them with a certain vitality, others doomed in advance to degenerate or ultimately to be destroyed.

In drawing up the balance sheet, therefore, one finds that the credit side is far from impressive considering the accrued costs of regional animosity, covert and overt, alienation from world opinion, whose support is still necessary for Israel, and the hundreds of dead and thousands of wounded in a war whose necessity has become increasingly doubtful. The economic balance during the past few years is also not particularly impressive. During the 1950s, 1960s, and also the early 1970s private consumption used up a large portion of the national product, some say too large, but it is a peculiarity of the late 1970s and early 1980s that consumption has been growing at the expense of an increased deficit in the balance of payments: loans taken out by the government (or guaranteed by it) in the international financial market have subsidised the increase in consumption. At the time of writing it is agreed that private consumption must be cut by as much as $2–2.5

billion a year in order to restore the balance of payments, this figure being based on the assumption that the United States will continue to provide loans and grants intended, in principle, to assist with the burden of defence. To illustrate the magnitude of the task, this cut is equal to close on 20 per cent of what is spent annually on private consumption.

Making a cut of this size is difficult in the best of circumstances and threatens more than a few social shocks. It is many times harder with three-digit inflation in the background. Inflation was accelerated by the change in economic policy instituted at the start of Shamir's Government. Reduction in the foreign trade deficit means a reduction in the supply of goods and services in the Israeli market. One need not be an economic expert to understand that if an increase in supply depresses prices, removal of part of that supply has the opposite effect. In other words, the problem of inflation, when it must be dealt with simultaneously with an acute balance of payments crisis, is particularly difficult to solve, the more so given the system of linkages in force in Israel, practically ensuring that any rise in price is automatically rolled over in salaries and linked investments.

The Economy

Economic development — and there is no doubt that the Israeli economy deserves to be called developed, both in terms of what it is capable of producing and of the scope and patterns of use by individuals and society — involves increased rigidity; the flexibility exhibited by the economy in leaping from the recession of 1966 to the boom of 1967 and 1968 is probably a thing of the past. Moreover, it is no longer certain that the public will again resign itself to a recession with the relative calm it showed in 1966, should a return to a deflationary policy be dictated by events as it was at that time in Israel and as has been the case since the beginning of the 1980s in most countries of the West.

The belief that it was possible to manage the economy in ways different from those employed during the three decades preceding the rise of the Likud has been shaken. The use of new control mechanisms, such as a floating exchange rate, the emphasis placed on the stock exchange as an independent source of investment capital, and the parallel retreat from the government's position as the guide of economic development — all these failed to yield satisfactory results. Thus, for example, a short time after they were implemented, the rules for floating the sheqel were changed. The ministers who launched the float had expected a flight of capital, and they had probably prepared means for preventing it. In fact, the opposite took place, and the sheqel began to gain strength. It was only later that they realised that, for reasons of comprehensive economic guidance, the government had to intervene, in order to control the inflow and outflow of funds, and that this had to be done by instituting what is called in the jargon, dirty floating.

As for the stock exchange, between 1977 and 1981 it worked satisfactorily as a financial market for the raising of investment capital. But in 1982 that market lost contact with reality: a mad boom developed which turned it into a casino where the main game, guessing future share prices, became the determining factor, as opposed to the asset value or other economic criteria. The boom continued for a year, followed by a market crash that wiped out half the value of the so-called free shares within six months. Towards the end of 1983 a second crash occurred. Bank shares had been manipulated by the issuing institutions until their prices on the stock exchange came to be double (as measured by the investment criterion known as the multiplier) or treble (according to the price-earnings ratio) their actual value. Now they were about to collapse because the banks no longer had the resources necessary to bolster the value of their own stock by purchasing excess supply. With the second crash, something unforeseeable took place: the government agreed to save the situation by means that were thought to be extinct. Politicians and bank executives agreed to convert the bank shares, the ownership of which implied unlimited risk, into government-backed bonds, the ownership of which entailed minimal risk. The technique by which this conversion was effected is less important in the present context than the fact that, in order to solve a market problem, the government resorted to means alien to an entrepreneurial regime, in which financial risk is an essential ingredient. Risk and profit are the two poles in the conceptual world of the entrepreneur: interest guaranteed by the government is the preferred method of encouraging savings in an economy administered along statist lines.

It must be pointed out that when the banks appealed to the government for help, they did not do so on business grounds, as did the Chrysler Corporation when it asked the US Government for a bridgeing loan of less than two years' duration in order to avoid bankruptcy. The aid requested — and we are dealing here with sums more than double those requested by Chrysler — was unilateral and not conditional on a return by the recipient; there was no give and take, merely give, exactly as was usual in the golden age of the Sapir economy. To translate what happened during the bank shares crisis into financial terms, the business sector requested and received an open-ended government guarantee of its business activities, both generally and in specific areas. Logic requires that they accept government guidance as the unavoidable consequence.

Under the Likud governments, especially after the appointment of Yoram Aridor as Minister of Finance, the government refrained from guiding economic development, that is, from shaping the future structure and capacities of the economy, or in other words the ability to produce and provide jobs and income under conditions of international competition. This task was left to entrepreneurs acting through the financial market, the stock exchange, and the banking system. The stock exchange and the banks are guided by considerations of short-term profit; they do not distinguish between initiatives which have general value and increase the competitive potential of the national economy, and those which rely on some temporary shift in the market, or whose profitability depends on special circumstances such as customs protection or transitory local advantage.

Some people attribute this characteristic of economic management under the Likud governments to the personalities of the Finance Ministers. However, that is putting the cart before the horse: the only similarity between the politicians appointed to this post, whether an easygoing man like Simha Ehrlich or a bully like Yoram Aridor, was their indifference to the shaping of tomorrow's economy. Both of them entrusted the function of planning investment to the business sector, whereas the Mapai Ministers of the Treasury, including those serving after their national agenda had been replaced following the Six Day War, viewed this as their most important task.

It has already been shown that in a crisis the rules of the economic game were simply put aside. A new economic reality came to light, different both conceptually and in practice from the one that had shaped the original rules, and which, as it turned out, suited the game only while the going was good. During the first decade and a half of its existence, it was assumed that centralised planning was the right way to structure and operate an economy in keeping with the needs of the state, and that it was possible to harmonise the economic actions taken by individuals through decisions made by government planners. This assumption was shown to be essentially mistaken during the recession of 1966. After the Six Day War a change began to take place — it should be emphasised that the process was a gradual one — which placed the main emphasis on entrepreneurial decisions; the government gradually faded into the background, and towards the end of the process, left the stage altogether. But the events of 1983 demonstrated that in a crunch the entrepreneurial system was not strong enough to stand on its own feet. What is no less interesting, the system was also not intellectually independent, for if it had been, it would not have requested unilateral government assistance, and would even have rejected such aid had it been offered.

The resolution of the economic crisis accompanying the transition to a new national agenda is conditional on a new synthesis between government planning and entrepreneurial management. The present-day entrepreneur is fairly well educated, experienced, and sufficiently self-confident to refuse to serve as the executive assistant of a minister or government bureaucrat. But for his own good he needs direction and someone to assume final responsibility for whatever actions are taken. The stock exchange and the financial system can provide him with money, but general goals, a stable framework for entrepreneurship, and assistance when difficulties arise must be looked for elsewhere. The division of labour between the government and the entrepreneur must be based on the particular characteristics of each party. The entrepreneur carries out the market survey and identifies a specific field of activity, but the government must tell him whether what he has chosen serves the national interest, for example, improving the balance of trade, or geographical dispersion, or providing employment, etc. The government must also make it clear to the entrepreneur just what assistance it is willing to provide, in what areas, what is the extent of its aid, and what is expected in return from the recipient. In principle, it is preferable that the assistance be given, if it is given, through entrepreneurial channels (for example, the purchase of shares by the governmental agency on the floor of the stock exchange or subscription to new issues). The Industrial Development Bank should be revived and turned into a prime source of capital in cases where the risk might seem excessive to investors on the stock exchange, although acceptable to the government. Without going into detail, it would seem that the relations between the government and entrepreneurs on the model of those prevailing between an investment bank (what is known in Britain as a merchant bank) and its clients would probably be best. In line with what has been described here, the budget would once again become an active element in investment policy to help finance initiatives that serve the national interest. Conceptually this would be tantamount to a return to the Sapir era, with modifications due to the much improved quality of management in today's firms, and to the government's computer-assisted ability to control and supervise.

The Emerging New Agenda

It is not difficult to offer further evidence of the exhaustion of the national agenda predicated on territorial expansion and the enhancement of Israel's international standing, and the government's withdrawal from economic activity. However, there is no reason to do so: anyone still unconvinced by what has been said so far, namely, that the term 'national agenda' identifies a significant variable providing a better understanding of political and social events in the past, and, to a degree, predicting the future, will not be convinced by further examples. Whatever the intellectual merits of the present argument, the time has now come to test its predictive power, with one self-explanatory reservation, however: external changes of the kind known as *force majeure* could easily throw the entire region into disarray, obliging Israel to adapt to them, even if doing so went counter to trends currently at work both within Israeli society and in the external environment.

For the present, which might be of short duration or last a few years, Israel is undergoing a change in its national agenda. At the end of the changeover emerging at present one can make out the outline of a new national agenda concentrated on domestic reform. Economics will dominate that national agenda, the concern with frontiers and Israel's international status taking second place, or at any rate a place less prominent than today. The reader who has followed the presentation of the central events of Israeli history in this essay, will easily perceive the striking similarity between the character of the national agenda between 1949 and 1967 and its predicted counterpart, as well as the difference, equally striking, between the guiding idea valid from the Six Day War until Menachem Begin's resignation (a rather convenient bench-mark) and the main features of the future agenda. Just as it did after the establishment of the state and the War of Independence, Israeli society will now concentrate on internal reform. In the first instance, this will be in response to contraints; the era of territorial expansion ended in an economic crisis which revealed Israel's dependence on external financing and endangered its sovereignty, the maintenance of its economic activity, full employment, a decent standard of living, and so on. Thus it appears that the sustained effort demanded to restore the situation, and the momentum which the public will have to gather for that effort, will place their stamp on the period before us and relegate other matters to the sidelines, or at least assign them a much lower place in the order of national priorities.

Two comments are in order here. The transition from the Mandate to national sovereignty was characterised by unbounded enthusiasm and the release of great energies that had been pent up within the nation. Spiritual exaltation and the sense of vast horizons opening up also marked the transition from the period of stagnation and the days of siege and mortal danger before the Six Day War to the era of victory and conquest which began immediately after it. In contrast, the present changeover is heralded by signs that Israel has come up against a blank wall in the political arena, and by doubts in the country's ability to achieve economic independence. Moreover, at least for the moment, there are no outstanding leaders or national heroes to lean on during hard times, to give direction to a confused nation that has lost its way. In short, for the period before us, there is no Ben-Gurion, no Dayan, and no Begin.

Although the nation suffers from lack of optimism and authoritative leadership at a time when it must gather strength for the leap forward, this deficiency is balanced by assets accumulated over the years since the establishment of the state. First of all, the most important of all these assets might be called — for lack of a better term — political persistence. In the years after the establishment of the state, Israel's neighbours reckoned they were dealing with a temporary entity which, through a combined political and military effort, including an economic boycott, could be wiped out once and for all. They therefore applied constant pressure, sometimes in the form of an all-out military effort meant to put an end to the alien body whose existence gave no rest to the Arab world. In the Arab states' estimate of the situation and the strategy they derived from it, time was the determining factor. The longer the foreign entity maintained its staying power under pressure and in war, the better it demonstrated the essential flaw in both the enemy's estimate and its strategy, thus obliging Israel's neighbours to relinquish them. In other words, by withstanding the continued tests to which it was subjected by its Arab neighbours, by defeating their armies in repeated wars, by creating a society and an economy and a firm network of relations with a super power and many other countries — all within three and a half decades — Israel posed a fundamental challenge to the Arabs' estimate of their chances of ridding themselves of the Jewish state. Just as the sense of Israel's temporary nature invited pressure and warfare, so withstanding pressure and persistence in the face of trials had the converse effect of weakening the hostile efforts of the kind made in the past. The results are evident: today Israel enjoys *de facto* peace with Jordan, *de jure* peace with Egypt, and something in between the two with Lebanon. No less important than these external signs of resignation to the Israeli existence, undesirable as they may find it, on the part of the Arab states, there are also signs of a resignation, however grudging, in their public opinion. Thus it can said that Israel has accomplished an historic achievement in its struggle with its Arab neighbours: it has made them re-examine their basic estimates of the situation, as well as the strategy adopted to achieve their goal. And even if, as many believe, the original goal has been retained in its essentials, a revision has been made with regard to the means appropriate to achieving it. From Israel's point of view, this is tantamount to the coming into existence of a wholly different political environment from that which preceded it, requiring a redirection of its efforts and a reallocation of its resources. This finding is consistent with the estimate that the main effort in the new national agenda will be directed towards domestic reform, especially in the economy. Israel can now — probably from now on — afford to concentrate its efforts internally, in the civilian arena, although it will certainly have to continue following events on the other side of its borders with vigilance.

The second asset is the economy itself. Although serious flaws in it have emerged recently, they derive mainly from management in need of improvement, perhaps even of a general overhaul. But this is not the same as starting from nothing. In thirty-five years an economy has come into being, parts of which can successfully meet the demands of the international market, particularly in the branches which are exposed to external competition or which supply the defence establishment. Here is one quantitative measure of the truth of this statement: in 1949 Israel probably did not export more than $100 million worth of goods; today annual exports total almost $11 billion. Admittedly, the dollar is not what it used to be, but a multiplier of 110 still serves as the reminder of an impressive success story. This achievement is the foundation upon which one can set the main pillar of the emerging national agenda, the essence of which will be the achievement of economic independence during the fourth and fifth decades of the state's sovereign political existence.

In plain English, economic independence means increased exports. In principle the production of goods and services to replace imports is equivalent to production for export. However, the scope for replacing imports by enhanced local production is quite narrow, owing to the limited scale of the Israeli market; in such circumstances it is preferable to exploit the competitive advantages implicit in the importation of goods which are mass-produced abroad, and to make an effort to pay for them out of income derived from the export of goods and services in which Israel has a relative competitive advantage. If it had general advantages, such as low wages relative to productivity, there would be no particular difficulty in identifying goods and services which should be produced in quantity in order to increase exports (although it is clear that the benefit derived from this advantage would increase as the proportion of wages per unit of production increased). However, Israel does not enjoy a comparative advantage of that kind. Therefore half the job, if not more, is to identify a market on the one hand, and products or services on the other, which can be sold optimally in it. The entrepreneur is charged with identifying markets and products. Thus he plays a major role in implementing the national agenda in what remains of the 1980s and thereafter. However, the entrepreneur cannot do his job well in conditions of unreasonable risk; consequently he might prefer to produce for the local market, which he knows well, and which he controls at least partially or, if he possesses a monopoly, completely. A favourable rate of exchange or other incentives are often insufficient to offset the risk assumed by the entrepreneur bent on selling abroad: hence the large Israeli trade deficit. Under the peculiar circumstances obtaining in Israel, no one except the government is strong enough to share that risk and exert sufficient pressure on the entrepreneur or tempt him to seek his fortune in foreign markets. Ideally what is needed here is a partnership in which the entrepreneur would scan the horizon for markets, if necessary with government assistance, and organise production and sales. In developed industrial economies the entrepreneur's partner is the institution that provides the funds, the bank, particularly the merchant bank. Its task is not limited to providing short-term loans; rather, it nurses the entrepreneur through the stages of project development, borrowing and raising capital in the stock exchange, setting up productive and marketing facilities, up to the point where he begins to make money. In Israel, the government, if it does place economic independence high on the new national agenda, will be called upon to act like a merchant bank. It will have to do more than create a favourable climate for exporters. Rather it must co-operate with the entrepreneur until the moment when he says 'enough' and declares that from now on he can stand on his own feet.

What has been described here should not be interpreted as a return to the system of Pinhas Sapir, under which the entrepreneur was little more than a sub-contractor to the government bureaucracy. Nor should it be seen as a mere sequel to the situation prevailing under the Likud, in which the entrepreneur does as he pleases and uses available sources of funds, the banks and the stock exchange, which are guided only by considerations of profit. The model to be borne in mind is the industrial organisation in Japan, or apparently in Singapore. Both these economies have been extremely successful due to the co-ordination of the activities of their leading companies with the governments, which see themselves as a combination of guide, partner in risk, assistant in development, raiser of capital, and marketing promoter. The more the government succeeds in making the economy into 'Israel, Ltd' on the Japanese model, the better it will advance the goal of economic independence.

One of the difficulties in creating a partnership between the government and entrepreneurs of the sort just described is rooted in the approach of the average bureaucrat. He views his task as planning (in the past) or supervision (always), within the framework of a budgeted, hierarchical, and generally restricted world of his own making. This also applies to bureaucrats with specific qualifications: economists, accountants, lawyers, etc. Businessmen have understood the need for developing a form of professional training especially suitable for those wishing to rise in the managerial hierarchy in business, commerce, and banking; business schools provide such goal-oriented training. But Israel does not possess educational institutions like the Ecole Nationale d'Administration (ENA) in France, particularly suited to people who see their future in the senior ranks of government and it certainly does not possess any special institution to train government administrators to fulfil the task described above, to be the actual partner of an entrepreneur and exporter. This deficiency must be remedied; the difficulty of accomplishing a pioneering task of this kind must not prevent the attempt from being made.

The establishment of an economic regime, as described above, could well move Israel forward on the path to economic independence. It does, however, contain an implicit danger of discrimination and arbitrariness. Exporters will receive benefits denied to other entrepreneurs, and among those who receive benefits some will receive more than others. We are dealing here with human affairs, and some discrimination and arbitrariness inevitably creeps in. All that can be done is to attempt to limit what is undesirable by opening government control to public inspection, knowing full well that that is no guarantee of perfection.

The events in the capital market during 1983, particularly during the second half of the year, and the decline in share prices as a permanent phenomenon, are open to two interpretations. According to one of them, that which falls will ultimately rise again; in other words, the stock exchange will revive and once again function as a source of capital for long-term investment. The other interpretation centres on the character of the activity which went on in the stock exchange; it came to resemble a casino, that is, the aspect of participation in a game of chance was effectively divorced from that of raising capital, the proper reason for the existence of a stock exchange. As long as the gambling encouraged lively activity, the capital-raising function was also served, although as an afterthought, as it were. But as the easy, tax-free capital gains dried up, the stock exchange ceased to function as a market for investment capital. In short, it could be said that in the Tel Aviv stock exchange the secondary became primary, and the primary secondary. Therefore, apart from transitory turns of events, it can no longer be counted on as a reliable source of investment capital. In fact, it was never meant to serve as the main source until the Likud governments came along and burdened it with a task beyond its strength. The Likud governments abandoned the accepted practice both for ideological reasons and because of the growing demands of current outlays at the expense of resources which, in the past, had been channelled to fund the development budget. During the period under discussion the rate of investment declined dramatically. Whether the decline was attributable to an autonomous shift of economic resources or to the worldwide economic recession, or whether it was a consequence of a reduction in the governmental supply of investment capital on preferred terms, as was the practice before the Likud took power, is a question which deserves further investigation. In any event, the stock exchange could not completely replace the budget as a source of investment capital, despite the attractions of the tax-free status of capital gains from investment in shares.

The conclusion that suggests itself here is that, in order to promote the raising of capital locally, the government must once again increase the share of the budget to finance development. This is consistent with what has been said above about the need to strengthen the government's role as the promoter and dependable partner of entrepreneurial activities aimed at foreign markets. Naturally, it is easier to point out and justify such a need than to act to satisfy it. Government budgets have always been stretched past breaking point, as both defence expenditures and debt services have greatly increased, and also deliberate government activity in the area of welfare. It is very difficult to point to items in the budget which can be reduced or excised in order to free funds for investment. However, competition for resources is the essence of economics, including competition between budgetary outlays on current expenses and capital investment. Suffice it to say here that, in order to implement the national agenda, future governments will have to channel certain resources into investment to help progress towards economic independence.

Another important issue of principle remains: the government's obligation to provide employment for all who wish to work. In Israel's early years this obligation appeared to be a Zionist commandment: the government was positively required to ensure the productivisation of the Jewish people in its homeland and the inversion of its pyramid of employment. The policy of providing employment at any price was, to no small extent, behind the creation of jobs for mere show. It produced anomalies within the

Israeli economy which continue to characterise it, and it is not at all clear that the continuation of this policy is consistent with the requirements of efficiency incumbent upon a national economy which has given the highest priority to balancing its foreign trade. These remarks do not refer merely to frictional unemployment, that is, unemployment deriving from the loss of certain jobs which no longer produce goods of competitive quality or price and which continues until the unemployed worker finds another job, more in keeping with market demand. By definition, frictional unemployment is transitory and thus not of great concern to a government seeking to reform the national economy over a period of years (although from the short-term point of view, unemployment is unemployment, and those who suffer from it have a claim to assistance). The unemployment we are discussing here derives from overstaffing, brought to light by increased efficiency in individual plants and in the economy as a whole.

What should be done with the unemployed, those who are thrown out of the process of production and who cannot adapt because of their age, location, or lack of training for the conditions imposed by an increasingly sophisticated economy? We have no ready answer to this question. But there is a principle to guide progress towards economic independence: one must not overload the productive process with social burdens. In other words, the obligation to provide full employment is not absolute. Therefore, if unemployment increases as a constant phenomenon during the years when the economy is striving for independence, the government must harden its heart and reconcile itself to the fact that a certain number of potential wage-earners — greater than has been tolerated up to now — will remain unemployed. As such, they will need to be supported by state and local welfare institutions.

A Possible Peace Policy?

Since 1967 Israel has concentrated on external matters which come under the general heading of foreign affairs and defence. Conversely, the emerging national agenda will concentrate on domestic, mainly economic, reforms. This is the active aspect, the field in which there must not only be achievements but achievements which are highly visible. But a load of unsolved problems hang round Israel's neck in the area of foreign affairs and defence, which will have to be dealt with if domestic reforms are to be carried out. The fact that between 1977 and 1981 Israel has spent an annual average of 20 per cent of available net resources (GNP plus net import capital) on defence makes any further explanation superfluous.

The assymetry of Israel's dispute with its neighbours lies at the root of its security problems, which are as old as the state itself. On the face of it, the Arabs lose only battles, never wars, whereas Israel knows that military defeat is liable to bring about the destruction of the Jewish state itself. Israel's strategic goal has therefore been to remove this assymetry or to reduce it: significant, perhaps decisive, progress has been made in this area since the War of Independence. Some people hold that hatred for Israel is the source of the conflict. However, hatred neither kills people nor destroys cities; in the worst case it makes it easier for the leaders of the Arab states, who have decided to wage war against Israel anyway, to mobilise support for their action among public opinion in their countries. Thus, Israeli policy need not be directed at reducing Arab hatred — although activity in that direction is desirable in itself — but rather it should see to it that the Arab heads of state, whose considerations are no less rational than those of other politicians, dispense with the idea of waging war. In other words, to remove the sting of the assymetry from the conflict by postponing or nullifying the military option would answer the strategic needs which circumstances have imposed upon Israel.

Some hold that the peace treaty with Egypt marks the settlement of the dispute between Egypt and Israel. This conclusion seems quite sound, although one should phrase it somewhat differently: today the Egyptians have no interest strong enough to justify going to war, even though war does not threaten their existence. Such an interest might emerge in the future, if the Israeli deterrent force became so weakened that making war against Israel, including war intended to wipe it out, seemed a trivial matter to the Egyptian leaders. But the chances that that might actually happen seem rather slim at the present time. It is not the peace treaty but rather the return of Sinai which has effectively removed the Egyptians from the group of actively hostile Arab states. In consequence, if Egypt remains outside that group, this will not necessarily be because it has joined a global system headed by the United States. Reconciliation with Israel is based on the settlement of the bilateral dispute between Egypt and Israel in a manner acceptable to Cairo.

It would appear, given the limited risks entailed, that Israel could afford to leave the disputes with Syria and Jordan unresolved. However, these disputes should be viewed in a broader perspective — the desire to divert the main national effort from the long-standing concentration of concern on foreign affairs and security issues to the area of domestic reform. There can be little doubt about the essentials of the solution: it means giving the Arabs political control over the West Bank and the Gaza Strip. To apply the model of autonomy tried in Poland between the two world wars is quite likely to end the way that autonomy ended, first in the division of Poland, and later on, as a result of a war in which Poland played no independent role, turning it into a national state by bodily moving it westward. Those who advocate, for security reasons, offering the Palestinians territorial autonomy within the framework of the State of Israel, base their opinion on a single assumption: that Jordan will continue to be actively hostile to Israel, even following the transfer of large parts of Judea, Samaria, and the Gaza Strip to its sovereignty. This assumption entirely or partially contradicts the assumption underlying the peace treaty with Egypt, which has already been put to the test during the war in Lebanon and has proved its advocates correct. Autonomy within the framework of the State of Israel does offer additional security, but in return it brings constant friction with the Arab population. Furthermore, the acceptance of civilian responsibility for that population, in the economy, in welfare, in culture, etc., would require the diversion of resources which are needed for other purposes far more important from Israel's point of view.

A purely Palestinian solution, that is, the establishment of a Palestinian state, is unthinkable since the Palestinian territorial claim is total and refers to the entire Land of Israel. Thus there is no room for compromise — the less so as the territory not in fact used by the Jews is insufficient for an independent Palestinian state. A rational Israeli policy would therefore work towards agreement with Jordan, including the transfer of sections of the Land of Israel to its control, either immediately or after a short transition period. A return to the Green Line (the 1949 armistice line) is also inconceivable: the Israeli public would not stand for it. On the other hand, even if Jordan were to agree in principle to a territorial compromise, it can do no other than reject the borders proposed by the Allon plan, which envisages an Arab enclave in Judea and Samaria entirely surrounded by Israeli territory. This peace plan, named after its initiator, the late Yigal Allon, is a clever gimmick rather than the sum of all political and military wisdom. The Jordan River does not constitute a boundary which is important for Israel's security, according to the book by Brigadier General Arieh Shalev, *A Line of Defence in Judea and Samaria.*[1] If the area transferred to Jordan were kept free of heavy weapons and if IDF observation and listening posts were emplaced on the crest of the hills under the terms of the agreement, Israel's security needs would have been met. Such an arrangement would hold even more if the Israeli border were moved a few kilometers to the east along its entire length, with a somewhat deeper bulge in the north of the West Bank. A significant part of the settlements established since 1967 would then be included within Israel's sovereign territory; the existence of the rest would depend on the agreement with Jordan and the willingness of the settlers to live under foreign rule.

Many people in Israel labour under a common delusion: that it is possible to resolve any political dispute in one go, either by advancing or withdrawing, depending on whether one views it from the right or the left. There are, however, disputes which are only settled after a great deal of time has passed, or which remain unresolved for ever. Israel's dispute with Syria seems to belong to the latter category, especially in view of the annexation of the Golan Heights and their having become a populated part of the State of Israel in every respect. The notion that it might be possible to compensate Syria by giving up control over part of Lebanon has at least two flaws: Israel has no effective control over Lebanon which it is able to give up; and Syria's political ties, especially with the Soviet Union and the PLO, make such an agreement impracticable. An agreement with Syria based on the exchange of the Golan for Lebanon would put the PLO back on Israel's northern border; and if Syria were to seek to prevent PLO activity from there, it would lose its legitimacy in the eyes of the Palestinian diaspora. However, the direct difficulty lies in Syria's imperial dreams, which impel it to take steps intended to weaken the Israeli and Jordanian governments: a pro-Syrian PLO is a tool for this purpose, and the PLO, based in Lebanon and controlled by Syria, can exist only if it remains subject to Syria and carries out its policies. In contrast, an agreement with Jordan, of the type mentioned above, would effectively make Israel Jordan's ally: the alliance would find expression, among other things, in Israeli assistance to Jordan to maintain the agreement between them and to protect Jordan's border with Syria.

One might say that in the proposed peace policy, which is also a policy for weaning Israel from its prolonged and obsessive concern with foreign affairs and defence, Israel must choose between a Jordanian or a Syrian orientation: the two are mutually exclusive. Presuming, of course, that there is a realistic choice between the two — which is not in fact so — Israel will therefore have to resign itself to Syrian hostility, at various levels of intensity as a long-term phenomenon. The price of this will necessarily be expressed in forms of Israel's military deployment, based on the assumption that the northern border is active and liable to erupt in warfare at very short notice. In any event, the contact line with Syria is liable to require continuous attention, approaching a state of constant military alert. In the foreign and military policy formula proposed for Israel, 'Obtain political settlements so that you may turn your back on the Arabs', relations between Jerusalem and Damascus cannot be included.

As noted above, Israel annually spends about 20 per cent of its net resources on security. Up to and including 1968 the figure was not even 10 per cent. An enormous military achievement like the victory in the Six Day War did not serve to reduce the defence burden. On the contrary; from 1967 on defence expenditures settled at around an annual average of 20 per cent of the total net resources available to the economy, a burden which was very hard to bear, and which, it seems, is no longer necessary. There are several reasons for this. The policy of agreements, which in the case of Egypt has already produced positive results, and which is likely to produce similar results in the Jordanian-Palestinian context, reduces the need for vigilance (which devours most of the resources). Israel has two further security assets, both of them on the strategic level, and each at a different stage of development, either of which could deter the Arabs from launching comprehensive military action against it.

Relations with the US

Since the late 1960s the United States has become Israel's main supplier of weapons; apart from this, it has financed the lion's share of the balance of payments deficit and provided political protection when needed. The American obligation, which Presidents of the United States have proclaimed on various occasions, was originally unilateral, but over the years it has changed somewhat and turned into a give and take relationship; the United States expects, and receives, a return for its assistance, either in information or in a degree of involvement whenever problems arise in which an Israeli stand or action might carry weight, either as a sovereign state or as the focus of the Jewish people. In one way or another a very special sort of relationship has developed between Israel and the Western superpower. This, if it were strengthened just a little more, would deter any other country, including the USSR, from using military force against Israel or, if the warning proved ineffective, would ensure logistical assistance in time of war, or even direct US involvement in the hostilities.

It is quite likely that if Israel made a serious effort to settle the question of its eastern border, relations with the United States would become much closer. The United States took it upon itself to achieve such a settlement as part of the efforts of President Carter to bring about the signing of the Egyptian-Israeli peace treaty, to which he attached a US guarantee. In view of this precedent, it is conceivable that, as part of an Israeli-Jordanian-Palestinian agreement, the United States would sign a defence treaty with Israel (perhaps in parallel with one with Jordan too). Something like a defence relationship between Israel and the United States already exists in fact, and is publicly known; the chances of formalising it in a treaty are quite good, especially against the background of the achievement of an American policy goal by settling the issue of Judea, Samaria, and the Gaza Strip. If there had been such a defence treaty, it is doubtful whether the Lebanese War would have been undertaken. Furthermore, an Israeli government which adapted its policies to the requirements of a national agenda principally concerned with domestic reform would not pose a difficult security problem for Washington.

The idea of striving for a defence treaty with the United States has already been discussed theoretically; and some convincing arguments have been raised against it. Two deserve closer consideration. One is that the signing of a defence treaty effectively cancels out Israeli sovereignty, in that it subjects its right to make war, even in self-defence, to the assent of its partner — when the right to go to war is the essence of sovereignty. The other argument is that Israel cannot count on the United States to fulfil its obligations, and that, even if it does fulfil them, the processes prescribed by American law would necessarily delay assistance so as to deprive it of any real value. The second of these objections has greater merit: the American Constitution stipulates that a congressional review of any treaty is decisive, in other words, the action of signing a treaty merely indicates the acceptance of conditional responsibility. However, during the Yom Kippur War it was shown that, without any defence treaty, the United States was prepared to offer logistical assistance with no bureaucratic delays. Moreover, inasmuch as the treaty would confirm an already existing common interest, it is likely that the promised military assistance would in fact be forthcoming. At the very least, any potential enemy would need to consider the possibility that the United States would honour its treaty obligations: its deterrent value is therefore indisputable. As for the argument about limiting Israel's sovereignty implicit in the right to make war, in fact, although the right to start a war does not at present depend on American approval, the ability to continue it certainly does. If anyone needs proof of that, let him simply look at what happened during the Sinai Campaign in 1956, the Yom Kippur War, and in Lebanon: all three wars were halted when the United States indicated that it was time to stop. Therefore, since Israeli sovereignty is limited in any case, to limit it in advance is no real concession.

Regardless of the problems inherent in a defence treaty with the United States, if the two sides were to sign one it would be likely to offer a partial substitute for budgetary outlays on defence. A defence treaty is not, however, the only substitute. For some time now Israel has had a nuclear option. But it is an option, as the late Haim Laskov said, like the Hanucca lights,[2] which are meant to be seen but never used. Others are of a different opinion, however. Several years ago Moshe Dayan proposed that the option be acknowledged, that is, revealed and, of course, included among the weapons at Israel's disposal, either to make the enemy see and beware, or else to be used in time of extreme danger. In other words, Dayan regarded the Israeli nuclear capability, the existence of which he assumed, for the sake of argument, as a deterrent, but also as a military potential, i.e. as a substitute for other defence resources which could be dispensed with thanks to the nuclearisation of Israeli strategy. Others have made similar proposals, and recently Dr Shai Feldman of Tel Aviv University published a book, *A Nuclear Deterrent for Israel*,[3] which analyses the subject in detail and offers a well reasoned and fully documented proposal for basing Israel's strategy on nuclear weapons, both because of the effectiveness of nuclear deterrence and because of its relatively low cost.

It is quite likely that in the foreseeable future Israel will not be able to combine a defence treaty with the United States and the adoption of a strategy of nuclear deterrence, since this would be inconsistent with the US aim of preventing the proliferation of nuclear weapons. A choice between the two must therefore be made. Some would prefer nuclear deterrence since it does not entail either dependence on US willingness to help Israel in time of war or a concession of sovereignty. However, self-reliance and insistence on complete and unquestioned sovereignty carry a big price tag: the actual decision to use nuclear weapons is an extremely difficult one, particularly if the political leadership is not sufficiently determined, or if there is some doubt as to whether they have convinced their own people and the enemy that they are prepared to go to the limit. There is also the argument that human beings should not be saddled with the awesome responsibility of using such destructive weapons. Whoever acquires nuclear deterrence also acquires a unique phsycological and moral burden. It must be remembered that a country which bases its security on nuclear deterrence and, when necessary, the use of nuclear weapons, and then fails to convince itself and others of its resolution to carry that strategy to the bitter end, is actually betraying its security.

In concluding this brief survey of the options open to those wishing to reduce the burden of defence expenditures, we must recall the general political framework in which the choice will be made. The objective is the transfer of public attention inwards, to strengthen the country's economic muscle and improve its social functioning, to reduce tensions among its citizens and to create a more decent relationship between the individual and the national government, professional unions, and local authorities. Without denying the importance of the security of borders and lines of defence in the new national agenda neither will possess the existential value attributed to them since 1967. The circumstances which justified devoting the main resources of the state to them and, as a corollary, giving Israel's international status highest place in the national order of priorities no longer exist. From now on Israeli policy is likely to be essentially defensive, which is likely to blunt the sting of an American-Israeli defence treaty or the adoption of a nuclear strategy, no matter which is chosen. Once the decision is made regarding a territorial settlement on Israel's eastern border along the lines sketched above, and consequently only Israel's northern border with Syria remains active, two tasks will remain for the managers of Israel's foreign policy: the taking of preventive diplomatic measures against anything liable to upset the peace, and the promotion of foreign trade.

We have now presented the main outlines of Israel's national agenda for the next decade and a half. Some people might argue that the proposed agenda ignores certain topics which are unavoidable in any discussion of Israeli politics. To mention just two of them: is it not an error to neglect the problem of ethnic groups, the so-called social gap and its accompanying tensions, the solution of which must be accorded a high national priority? And can any serious discussion of the Israeli economy afford to ignore inflation?

The omission of the Ashkenazi-Sephardi problem in the above agenda was intentional. Tensions exist in any society: their origins can be ethnic, class-based, or cultural. The relevant question here is whether the tensions place their stamp on society or whether they are secondary to other issues of greater intensity. For example: there is the preoccupation with race in present-day South Africa; there were the religious wars of seventeenth-century Europe and the class struggle of nineteenth-century materialism. There can be no comparison between these dominant social conflicts and the controversy bearing on ethnic differences between Ashkenazis and Sephardis in contemporary Israel.

Inflation is essentially a cop-out of governments which have failed to achieve a reasonable balance between their expenditures and revenues. It now appears that the Israeli Government is on the way to correcting its profligate spending habits. But it is a truism that the stabilisation of the purchasing power of the country's currency is secondary to a general solution of its main economic problems particularly to the achievement of economic independence, that is, to getting the economy to stand on its own feet. A national agenda centred on domestic reform will therefore include dealing with inflation, but subject to the dictates of the principal economic goal, the achievement of economic independence — without entering here into a discussion of the precise meaning of that phrase.

Politicians are not free to choose a national agenda. Their job is to serve as the midwife to an agenda which answers to the public's sense of its needs. The ability to identify the ingredients of a national agenda and to formulate and implement it sets apart politicians of stature: parties led by men blessed with this gift and which identify themselves with the dynamic of a given national agenda have a good chance of taking power and retaining it for a long time.

Notes

1. Arieh Shalev; *A Line of Defence in Judea and Samaria* (Hebrew) (Hakibutz Hameuhad, Centre of Strategic Studies, Tel Aviv, 1982).

2. Hanucca is the feast of lights, commemorating the victory of the Maccabees over the Syrians in the second century BC and the rededication of the Temple.

3. Shai Feldman, *A Nuclear Deterrent for Israel* (Hebrew) (Hakibutz Hameuhad, Tel Aviv, 1983).

INDEX